The Kids' Book Club

Book Club

Member

The Kids' Book Club

Lively Reading and Activities for Grades 1–3

Desiree Webber
and
Sandy Shropshire

Illustrated by Sandy Shropshire

2001
Libraries Unlimited
A Division of Greenwood Publishing Group, Inc.
Englewood, Colorado

*To the authors and illustrators
who graciously shared their time and stories.*
—DW

*For those who share the joy of
books and literature with children.*
—SS

⅋

LIBRARIES UNLIMITED
A Division of Greenwood Publishing Group, Inc.
P.O. Box 6633
Englewood, CO 80155-6633
1-800-237-6124
www.lu.com

Library of Congress Cataloging-in-Publication Data

ISBN 1-56308-818-5

Contents

List of Figures

Figure

FIGURE

Preface

How do we instill a love of reading in our children? By sharing quality books and introducing the talented individuals who write and illustrate them. Book discussions and activities such as games, crafts, and puzzles also develop a deeper appreciation of the story.

Host a book club in your library or classroom, and you will see children devouring books. For forty-five to sixty minutes each week, children will have an opportunity to express their viewpoints, be creative, thoughtful, and engaged. Everyone, including you, will have a great time. Nothing can be more thrilling than seeing children learn—and enjoying the process.

Reading clubs are not new, but many reserve this activity for students in fourth grade and higher. *The Kids' Book Club: Lively Reading and Activities for Grades 1–3* is designed for public librarians, media specialists, and teachers working with children in first through third grades. The authors developed this book after many years of conducting successful book clubs for emerging and beginning readers.

The first chapter gives information on planning and implementing a successful book club. It covers suggestions for publicity, obtaining multiple copies of the books to be read, discussion guidelines, an introductory letter to parents, and what to do at that first meeting with the children. The remaining fifteen chapters provide book discussion sessions complete with questions, author and illustrator biographies from personal interviews, worksheets, games, activities, and crafts for you to conduct innovative reading clubs in your library or classroom.

It is the authors' hope that your book clubs are rewarding and enjoyable experiences. It is a thrill to see children brimming with enthusiasm as they arrive for the book club meeting. As the young people participate in the activities and voice their opinions during the discussion, you know that you are developing a lifelong appreciation for reading and learning.

CHAPTER 1

How to Plan and Conduct a Successful Book Club

When six-, seven-, and eight-year-olds enthusiastically attend a program week after week, you know that you have a hit. That is what librarians and teachers will experience with these book club sessions.

Each week children will arrive eager to discuss that week's title. They will interact with one another. They will talk and listen. They will want to play the games, make the crafts, and solve the puzzles. They will want to learn—and read, and read, and read.

The Kids' Book Club: Lively Reading and Activities for Grades 1–3 will help you plan and implement your own successful reading club for first- through third-grade children. Within this chapter are instructions for planning and conducting your first meeting, moderating a book discussion, acquiring multiple copies of books, implementing registration, handling publicity, and much more. Following this chapter are fifteen book discussion sessions ready for you to conduct with ease.

What Is a Book Club?

A book club is a program for readers to gather, discuss a book, and participate in related games and crafts. It introduces children to the concept of reading for pleasure, and that cannot happen too early.

The program can take place at the public library after school or in the evening. During the summer it can be offered mornings, afternoons, or evenings. A reading club can also take place at the school media center or in the classroom. In whatever setting *The Kids' Book Club* is implemented, the joy of reading and literature is realized.

Normally, the children meet once a week at a regularly scheduled time. For first through third grade, a book club session should last forty-five to sixty minutes. Include the first through third graders together in the program. The younger children will learn from the older ones, and if a third grader is struggling with reading, he or she will not feel out of place because many of the first graders are just learning to read.

During the hour, the adult moderator serves snacks, introduces the author and illustrator, guides the book discussion, and leads the children in games and crafts using the fully developed plans in each of the following fifteen chapters. The hour moves at a smooth and brisk pace. Children enjoy the variety and are constantly engaged.

Why a Book Club for Grades 1–3?

Book discussion activities are often reserved for children in fourth grade and higher. *The Kids' Book Club: Lively Reading and Activities for Grades 1–3* will demonstrate that first through third graders benefit from reading clubs. They learn to think and formulate answers. They develop verbal skills to express themselves. During the sessions, the children are also introduced to art and music, and the group learns to interact in a positive, encouraging environment. Young readers are having so much fun they do not realize that they are developing important, lifelong literacy skills.

Marcia Freeman, author of *Building a Writing Community: A Practical Guide* (Maupin House, 1995), writes, "We immerse children in language, talking to babies before they can speak. We demonstrate language, pointing to objects and repeating words. We fully expect that children will talk. . . . We tolerate their approximations, accept their misspeaking, and continue to provide models. . . . We do not make children feel threatened and thus inhibited about their speech."

These are the conditions for a successful book club. The enjoyment of reading for pleasure and having fun together is foremost. Children will learn and blossom. The reward is seeing children checking out more books and discussing with excitement what they have read.

How to Plan a Kids' Book Club

It is recommended that book club sessions be held weekly at a regularly scheduled day and time for a set number of weeks. For example, the book club will meet each Thursday evening, 7:00–8:00 P.M., during the month of October. Ideally, a series of four to six sessions is good but no less than four weeks. It is best to have too few sessions with the kids requesting more than to have too many sessions and experience a dwindling attendance because other activities are calling for their attention.

Advertise the program several weeks in advance and ask the children to pre-register. Use flyers, posters, letters to parents, and press releases to area newspapers and radio stations to announce the event.

Have copies of the books that will be discussed on display for the children, parents, or teachers to review. When the children register for the book club, record their name, address, and telephone number. Make sure to write the parent's or guardian's name and work number, if the latter is relevant. During registration, give each participant a copy of the book to be discussed at the first session. Instruct them to read the book before they attend the first program. Take the time to make a reminder call the day before the first meeting, and speak to the adult who registered the child.

Address information is needed for sending a follow-up letter to the parent or guardian. Parents or guardians can discuss the contents of the letter and help prepare their children for the upcoming reading club. The letter should be sent on the library's or school's letterhead. A sample letter to the parent or guardian follows (Figure 1.1, page 4).

Obtaining Multiple Copies of the Books to be Read

Gathering multiple copies of each title takes pre-planning. If you have access to a library system, enough copies of needed titles may exist. Allow four weeks to place reserves and to have the titles arrive. Otherwise you will need to purchase the books.

If at all possible, work toward building a book club collection. The expense is justified because these sessions can be repeated in the future with a new set of children. The titles will be used numerous times.

Request financial support from your administration, Friends of the Library, PTA, or library/school foundation. If these options are not available, seek funds from one or more community businesses or civic groups.

Whenever you approach an organization for funding, be prepared to describe the program. Emphasize the benefits to children and how much funding you will need. Many of the titles recommended in *The Kids' Book Club* are available in paperback, but weigh the longevity and use factor in considering whether to purchase the hardcover edition. Remember to include the costs for craft supplies, and emphasize the importance of extending activities to improve the learning impact.

If writing or speaking to a business or civic group, tell them how they will be thanked and acknowledged for their contribution. For example, suggest that each book be stamped on the inside front cover with "Donated by the First National Bank for the Clayton Public Library Book Club!" Be sure to ask for enough money to cover the cost of purchasing the stamp.

[date]

Dear Young Reader and Parent/Guardian:

What is a book club? It is a literature program involving a group of boys and girls all reading the same book and discussing it in a scheduled session. An appreciation of fine literature, the development of broadened areas of reading interest, and an improvement of reading skills are some of the desired goals. Through sharing ideas with others in the group, each young person will be stimulated to make effective use of critical thinking, learn to respect the opinions of others, and communicate more clearly.

Books to be read and discussed will be chosen from children's book award winners, fantasy, poetry, biography, historical fiction, and nonfiction. We recommend that adults read and enjoy these works with the child, and begin discussion at home. The insights you and your child may share in this exchange of ideas could be invaluable.

The group will meet the four Thursday nights in October at 7:00 P.M. Each participant must have read the book due for discussion each week. Adults should encourage their child to read the book early in the week, assisting him or her in time management so that the book can be completed. Please be on time or early so that all the planned activities can be covered within the short one-hour session.

The adult leader of the book club program acts as a moderator only. The role of the leader is to guide the discussion to important concepts, help the children stay on the subject at hand, and encourage everyone in the group to participate.

A modest snack will be served. The snacks will match the theme of the program and can be anything from pita bread and cheese to birthday cake and punch. Please let me know if your child has any food sensitivities or restrictions. You may want to make arrangements to send along an alternative.

We hope this experience will be an enjoyable one for your child with the chance to make new friends who love to read and talk. If at any time you have questions or comments, please do not hesitate to call.

For reading fun,

Sandy Shropshire
Discussion Moderator

P.S. Don't forget your library card!

Figure 1.1. Sample Introductory Letter

After you have received your donation, thank the donor with a press release to the newspaper along with a photograph of the first book club meeting. Post a big thank-you in the lobby and create a thank-you bookmark to send home with the children.

Setting up the Room

Evaluate the room where you are planning to hold the book club sessions. The children need to be seated at a table (or several tables put together) so that they are facing one another. This creates an environment conducive to sharing and getting to know one another better.

A table for snacks and displaying books for checkout is also needed. There needs to be an area indoors or outside for playing the games, such as "Take Me out to the Ballgame Musical Chairs," "Apple Head Relay," and "Portuguese Hopscotch."

If possible, decorate the room to emphasize reading or each book's theme. Request posters from book publishers, and display the authors' and illustrators' photographs. Showing photographs of the authors and illustrators brings an added dimension to the book discussion. It tells children that people just like them and their family members created beautiful, wonderful, thought-provoking books. It is possible that someday they can grow up and accomplish a similar artistic endeavor.

Number of Participants

A group of twelve to sixteen children is ideal for a book discussion group. It is large enough to have a diversity of ages, interests, and opinions and small enough for everyone to have an opportunity to talk. If you are planning to conduct a book club session in your classroom, divide the class into two or more groups to discuss the questions. As the adult moderator, move around the room to see if the children need to keep on track, or have a classroom aide or volunteer assist you by sitting with the additional groups.

Corresponding with the Authors and Illustrators

Use the contact information given at the end of each author's and illustrator's biographical information. Write several weeks in advance and tell the individual that you will be sharing one of their titles. Ask if he or she can send a letter for you to read to the book club group. (Tell them how many children will be in the club.) Sometimes authors and illustrators have time to send a signed photograph or a special letter that is unique and fun to share. Return postage is always appreciated when a response is requested.

Conducting the First Book Club Meeting

✓ **SUPPLIES**

Nametags

14-by-17-inch sheets of colorful construction paper
(one sheet per child)

Stickers

Markers or crayons

One roll of toilet paper

Prepare nametags for each meeting. If you have access to a button maker, buttons make the best nametags. Refer to Figure 1.2 for a nametag pattern. Write each child's first name on bright paper and add stars or other small stickers. Ask the children to return their nametags after each session for reuse at the following meeting. At the end of the last program, invite them to take their nametags home with them. Some children will save up several nametags as mementos for each reading club of which they were members.

Welcome each child as he or she arrives. At the first session, have the children make simple folders in which to keep handouts. Instruct them to place the 14-by-17-inch piece of construction paper in front of them, fold it up two inches from the bottom, and crease the edge. Staple the two ends. This creates a narrow pocket at the bottom edge for holding papers. Fold the paper in half lengthwise. The children should have a booklet that measures 8½ by 12 inches. Ask the group to write their names on their folders and to decorate with stickers, markers, or crayons.

Give children five to ten minutes to complete this activity. When finished, introduce yourself and invite all to get their snacks and return to their seats. Once everyone is seated, play the toilet paper game while they eat. This is a great icebreaker. The children meet and learn something about one another.

Toilet Paper Game

Pass around a roll of toilet paper. Tell the children that they can tear off one to ten sheets of toilet paper. It is up to them to choose how many sheets they want to take.

After everyone has selected their number of sheets, the moderator takes six. Tell the children that they have to tell something about themselves for each sheet of toilet paper they took. For example, they can talk about pets, brothers and sisters, and favorite games, books, or movies.

Figure 1.2. Book Club Nametag

The adult moderator starts the game. As you talk, tear off each sheet as you share something about yourself. For example:

1. My name is Ms. Myers.

2. I have a dog named Maggie and three cats named Tornado, Domino, and Itty-Bit.

3. My favorite book is *The Giver* by Lois Lowry.

4. I enjoy cross-country skiing.

5. I like to grow flowers.

6. I enjoy watching soccer—especially, the World Cup Games.

This game elicits a lot of laughs and gives everyone, even the shyest person in the group, an opportunity to speak.

When you have finished the game, introduce the book that everyone is prepared to discuss. For example, a good title to begin with is *Digging Up Dinosaurs* by Aliki. Tell the children about this author and illustrator and show her photograph from *The Kids' Book Club*. Tell the group that they will discuss the book and then make the Dinosaur Noodle Skeleton (Figure 5.2, page 64).

Before starting the group's first book discussion, give the children an idea of how it will be conducted and go over the Book Discussion Guidelines. Tell them that the questions for *Digging Up Dinosaurs* are on the back of the Triceratops graphic (Figure 5.1, page 60). The questions will be passed around in a small basket. The first child will select a dinosaur from the basket, read the question aloud, and give his or her answer or opinion. (If needed, give assistance when children are reading their questions and appear stuck at sounding out a word.)

Only one question will be drawn at a time. This keeps everyone focused on the question at hand. If a child does not want to answer the question, he or she can open it up to the group.

It is important that the tone for the book club be set at the first meeting. Children will want to know if they are going to be ridiculed for making a mistake while reading or when answering questions. Be lavish with praise, and set a tone of fun and enjoyment. Squelch any rude comments firmly but politely.

The following are the book discussion guidelines to be shared with the group. In addition to going over them verbally with the group, enlarge Figure 1.3, page 9, on colored photocopy paper, attach the guidelines to poster board, and set them on an easel. Make them visible at each meeting.

BOOK DISCUSSION GUIDELINES

Speak so that all can hear.

Talk to the group rather than the group leader.

Volunteer to speak without being called upon.

Avoid interrupting one another.

Talk only long enough to make your point.

Be willing to answer questions of others.

Discuss the book of the week. In other words, stay on the subject.

HAVE FUN!

Figure 1.3. Book Discussion Guidelines

Description of Chapters 2–16

Following this introductory chapter are fifteen prepared book club sessions. Each chapter has introductory information, biographies and photographs of the book's author and illustrator, sixteen discussion questions, a variety of activities to choose from, suggested snacks to serve, and a bibliography of related titles.

For each focus book there are more activities than can be used in one hour. This gives latitude in choosing what will be appropriate or of interest either to the librarian or to the children attending the program.

If the book club sessions are being held in a school setting, work with other educators in presenting the many activities available for each book. For example, the school media specialist can serve the snacks, introduce the author and illustrator, and conduct the book discussion. The art teacher can lead the craft, and the physical education teacher can teach the game. The puzzles and other handouts may be sent home for children to share with family members.

Some may hesitate at serving snacks during these sessions. Food serves as an icebreaker and can be viewed as a special treat for participating in the reading club. In addition, it can also be part of the learning process. For example, in the session for *Buffalo Thunder*, children will make butter like the early pioneers did. The homemade butter can be enjoyed with cornbread, pinto beans, and a glass of sarsaparilla. Enlist the assistance of parents, volunteers, and other staff in preparing the simple food items.

"Other Titles to Share" was included with each chapter so that related titles can be shared with the children. Make related titles available for checkout at each book club session. If children enjoy the topic, they will want to take other books home to read. For example, after sharing *Commander Toad and the Space Pirates* by Jane Yolen and illustrated by Bruce Degen, children may want to read the other titles in the series or read other books by Yolen and Degen.

Contact each of the publishers' marketing departments in advance. Tell them that you will be discussing one of their books and ask what complimentary promotional items they have to send you. Often there will be bookmarks, posters, and author and illustrator biographies for them to send. Request enough to share with each book club participant. For example, if the book club has sixteen members plus the moderator, ask for at least seventeen copies—one for each child plus one for the moderator's files.

In Conclusion . . .

The most important ingredient for a successful book club session is to *have fun*. The activities included in *The Kids' Book Club: Lively Reading and Activities for Grades 1–3* are designed to make reading more enjoyable. As the moderator, set the tone, be prepared, and let the children explore, learn, create, and discover how much pleasure there is in reading books. The result is a habit that will stay with them for life, along with an improved ability to learn, think, and speak.

CHAPTER 2

Black Cowboy, Wild Horses: A True Story

By Julius Lester

Illustrated by Jerry Pinkney

Lester, Julius. *Black Cowboy, Wild Horses: A True Story*. Illustrated by Jerry Pinkney. New York: Dial Books, 1998. [40 pages]

A true story about cowboy Bob Lemmons bringing a herd of wild mustangs to the ranch.

Introduction

The era of the cowboy began after the Civil War ended. Between 1867 and 1889, cowboys herded Longhorn cattle from Texas to states north, west, and east—wherever there were buyers hungry for beef. To drive cattle, each cowboy needed several mounts to make the trip northward. Ranchers assigned eight to fourteen horses per cowhand. During roundup time, horses were worked hard and fresh mounts were needed.

A cowhand's life was rough but colorful. He rode the range in all types of weather and at all times of the day and night. He roped cattle, broke horses, and branded a mark of ownership on both. To ward off loneliness, he told stories and sang songs. As a group, cowboys developed their own use of language, creating such expressive phrases as, "the snakes were so thick there you'd have to parade 'round on stilts to keep from gettin' bit."

Black Cowboy, Wild Horses tells how ex-slave Bob Lemmons develops an extraordinary talent for reading tracks and animals. Readers will be fascinated by the talent Lemmons exhibits in bringing in a herd of wild mustangs led by Warrior, his own black stallion.

11

As the children arrive, serve snacks and pass out the Cowboy Letter-Matching Game (Figure 2.2). Play music with songs depicting the old West, such as the audio compact disc, *I'm an Old Cowhand* by Bing Crosby (Living Era series, ASV Ltd., 1995, 1 Beaumont Avenue, London W14 9LP). Once everyone has gathered, play the Tossing Horseshoes game (see pages 18–20). Follow this activity with the introduction of the author and illustrator and then discuss the book.

Another option would be to proceed with the introduction of the author and illustrator, conduct the discussion of the book, and end with the Create a Branded Kerchief Craft (pages 21–22).

Introducing the Author and Illustrator

Julius Lester

Photo by Milan Sabatini. Courtesy of Dial Books for Young Readers.

Black Cowboy, Wild Horses is a picture-book version of a story that Lester took from his book *Long Journey Home: Stories from Black History* (Dial Books, 1993, 1972). It is the true story of how Bob Lemmons, an African American cowboy, brought in a herd of wild mustangs on his own. Lester is dedicated to telling stories of and about the Black experience in America.

"What I admire most [about Bob Lemmons] is that he was able to make wild horses believe that he was a horse," says Lester. "I wish I could have such a relationship with nature. It is such an incredible story and it is true. I wanted to share it with a younger audience."

Lester collaborated with Jerry Pinkney on *Black Cowboy, Wild Horses* after they both discovered a shared interest in African American cowboys of the American West. The two artists possess a mutual respect and admiration for the other's talents. When asked which illustration in *Black Cowboy, Wild Horses* is his favorite, Lester replies, "I don't know that I have a particular favorite. Each one has its own particular feel and quality. What I admire most in all of them is that Jerry painted the horses as individuals so that the horses you see the first time he depicts the herd are the same horses you see at the end. Each horse is individual and Jerry carried that individuality throughout the entire book, which I find incredible!"

Lester was born on January 27, 1939 in St. Louis, Missouri but grew up in Kansas City, Kansas and Nashville, Tennessee. Before writing for children, Lester wrote books and articles for adults. In 1968, his first children's book *To Be a Slave* (Dial), illustrated by Tom Feelings, was published. The book won a Newbery Honor Book citation. In 1994, his *John Henry* (Dial), illustrated by Jerry Pinkney, was a Caldecott Honor Book.

"I enjoy writing for all ages," says Lester. "I did not set out to become a children's book writer. It came about accidentally when I was introduced to Phyllis Fogelman who was a children's book editor at Dial Books at the time. I had been collecting narratives of former slaves and had been thinking about doing a book about what slavery was like from the point of view of the slaves. Phyllis liked the idea. The book was *To Be a Slave* and was the 1969 Newbery Honor Book. I was very fortunate that my first book for children received such recognition, and that recognition encouraged me to continue writing for children."

Lester is currently a professor of Near Eastern and Judaic Studies at the University of Massachusetts. Although he does not visit schools, he says if he did he would give this advice to children, "Read, read, read."

Letters to Julius Lester may be addressed to Dial Books for Young Readers, Penguin Putnam, Inc., 375 Hudson Street, Third Floor, New York, NY 10014.

Jerry Pinkney

Photo by Myles Pinkney. Courtesy of Dial Books for Young Readers.

"As a child growing up, I went to the movies all the time," says Pinkney. "This was the late 1950s and Westerns were really big. As a young person, I played cowboys all the time. I didn't know about African American cowboys and that one out of three cowboys were Black or Latino. That was fascinating to me [later, as an adult]. Working with Julius Lester on *Black Cowboy, Wild Horses* grew out of my interest in the West and my cultural heritage."

Pinkney and Lester have worked together on many books. Out of that collaboration has grown a friendship and a tremendous respect for one another. It was during one of their conversations when the two discovered that they shared an interest in the American West. Pinkney sent Lester an African American history calendar, featuring Black cowboys, that he had created in the mid-1970s for Seagrams. Lester sent Pinkney a copy of his book *Long Journey Home*. Together the two decided to work on *Black, Cowboy, Wild Horses*. Pinkney says the project allowed him to delve into more detail on one character, Bob Lemmons, and to illustrate a herd of mustangs. "The horse is such a beautiful animal," says Pinkney. "In myth and in real life."

Before illustrating the herd, Pinkney had to study the habits of mustangs through film and photographs. How would a horse hold its ears and tail during a full gallop, at rest, or while eating? When asked about the painting of the colt being bit by a rattlesnake, Pinkney replies that the viewer connects with the action going on. That is why the colt is up-close, tumbling head over heels in the foreground of the illustration.

"I always loved drawing as I grew up," says Pinkney. "Art as a career . . . that came later in my life. As an African American, I did not have any role models. I attended a vocational school and studied commercial art. I just forged ahead."

In the early 1970s, Pinkney began illustrating children's books. Since then, he has created the artwork for numerous children's books and has received three Caldecott Honor Awards for: 1995—*John Henry* (Dial 1994), 1990—*The Talking Eggs* (Dial 1989), and 1989—*Mirandy and Brother Wind* (Knopf 1988). He also has received four Coretta Scott King Awards and two Coretta Scott King Honor Awards.

Pinkney and his wife Gloria, an author, live in Westchester County, New York. They have four grown children and seven grandchildren.

Letters to Jerry Pinkney may be addressed to Dial Books for Young Readers, Penguin Putnam, Inc., 375 Hudson Street, Third Floor, New York, NY 10014.

Discussion Questions

Make sixteen photocopies of the cowboy boot graphic (Figure 2.1) on light brown paper. Add details with a dark brown or black thin-tipped marker. Reproduce the discussion questions (page 16) on white paper. Cut and glue them to the back of the boot graphic. Laminate, if possible, and cut along the outlines of the boots.

For fun, use a cowboy hat to pass around the questions. The boots should be face up with the questions hidden from view. Have one child select a boot from the hat, read the question aloud, and give his or her opinion or answer. If desired, the discussion can be opened to the group for others to give their thoughts. Then the hat is passed to the next individual who repeats the process. Allow only one boot to be drawn at a time. This prevents others from reading and concentrating on their questions and not listening to what is being discussed.

Remember, some of the discussion questions have more than one answer, or there is no "right" answer. Children may voice a completely different response than expected.

Activities

Cowboy Letter-Matching Game

Photocopy the activity sheet game (Figure 2.2, page 17) for each child in the book club.

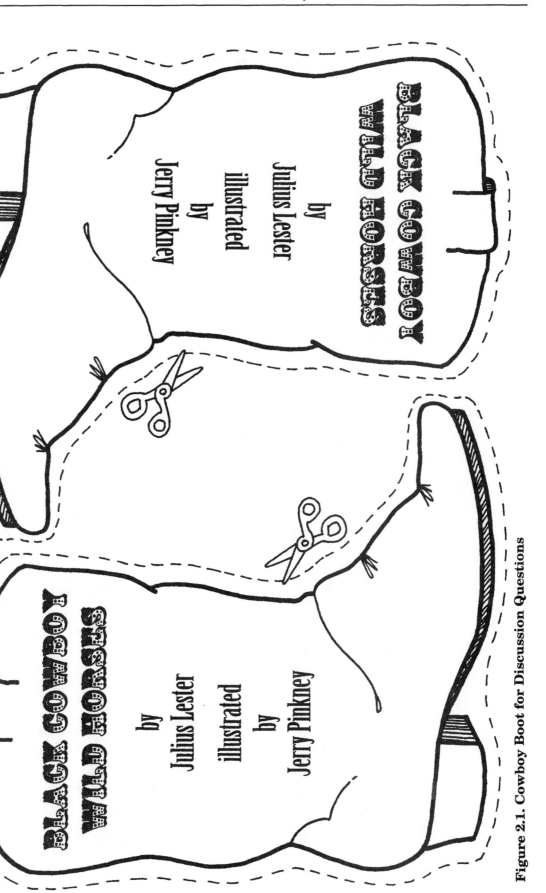

Figure 2.1. Cowboy Boot for Discussion Questions

Discussion Questions

What was the name of Bob Lemmons's horse?	What did Bob Lemmons learn from reading animal tracks?
Besides horses, what other animals appear in Pinkney's illustrations?	Why did the colt fall to the ground?
Why did Bob Lemmons leave the rattlesnake alone?	How did Bob Lemmons make himself one of the herd?
How did Warrior challenge the lead stallion?	Wild horses on the plains are called _____.
Which is your favorite illustration?	What did Jerry Pinkney draw in the clouds near the end of the book?
How did the cowboys react when Bob Lemmons brought the horses?	Would you like to be a cowhand? Why or why not?
Describe Bob Lemmons.	Where does the story take place— the mountains, plains, or beach?
Why had Bob Lemmons never learned to read?	What does Warrior want to do at the end of the story?

Cowboy Letter-Matching Game

Directions: Read each sentence. Sound out the word with the missing letter. Write in the correct letter to complete the word. Read *Black Cowboy, Wild Horses: A True Story* by Julius Lester, illustrated by Jerry Pinkney, to help you.

1. Bob Lemmons wore a co___boy hat.

2. Warrior was a black ___tallion.

3. Bob rode to the edge of the bl___ff.

4. Hawks ___lew in the sky.

5. Bob found hoof prints made by the ___ustangs.

6. Warrior liked to eat a___ples.

7. Bob drank from a cantee___.

8. Lightning streaked across the ___ky.

9. Bob wore a ___ancho.

10. There were ___ight mares.

11. The cowboys whoo___ed and hollered.

12. Warrior a___tacked the lead stallion.

Figure 2.2. Cowboy Letter-Matching Game

Tossing Horseshoes Game

✓ **SUPPLIES**

Heavyweight poster board

Cardboard or foamboard

Paper towel tubes

Glue sticks

Heavy-duty staples and stapler (for adult use only)

Cool glue gun (for adult use only)

Pads and pencils for keeping score (optional)

Making the Horseshoes

The adult moderator uses the horseshoe pattern (Figure 2.3, page 19) to create two horseshoes per team. A group of fifteen children, plus an adult, will make eight teams—each team consisting of two individuals. In this case, sixteen horseshoes would be needed.

Trace the horseshoe pattern on heavyweight poster board. Any color may be used, but each team needs to have a matching pair of horseshoes. For example, team A can have two red horseshoes and team B can have two blue horseshoes. If two teams have the same color, and they play against one another, draw some type of distinguishing mark to differentiate between the two pairs of horseshoes.

For each horseshoe needed, trace and cut out three horseshoes from the poster board. Using the glue stick, glue the three horseshoes together, one on top of the other. Once the glue has dried, use a heavy-duty stapler and staple around the horseshoe. The staples will add weight, making the horseshoe easier to toss, and will also keep the horseshoe from splitting apart during play.

Making the Horseshoe Pole

The adult moderator makes the horseshoe pole by cutting a piece of cardboard or foamboard 15 inches by 15 inches. To create the pole, take a paper towel tube and cut tabs to flare out and glue to the cardboard. To cut the tabs, use scissors and make half-inch deep cuts every three-fourths of an inch. Flare the tabs outward. The paper towel tube should be able to rest on a flat surface because the tabs act as a base. Glue the paper towel tube into place using the cool glue gun. It should be standing straight up to create the horseshoe pole (Figure 2.4, page 19). The horseshoe pole is what the students will toss their horseshoes at to score points.

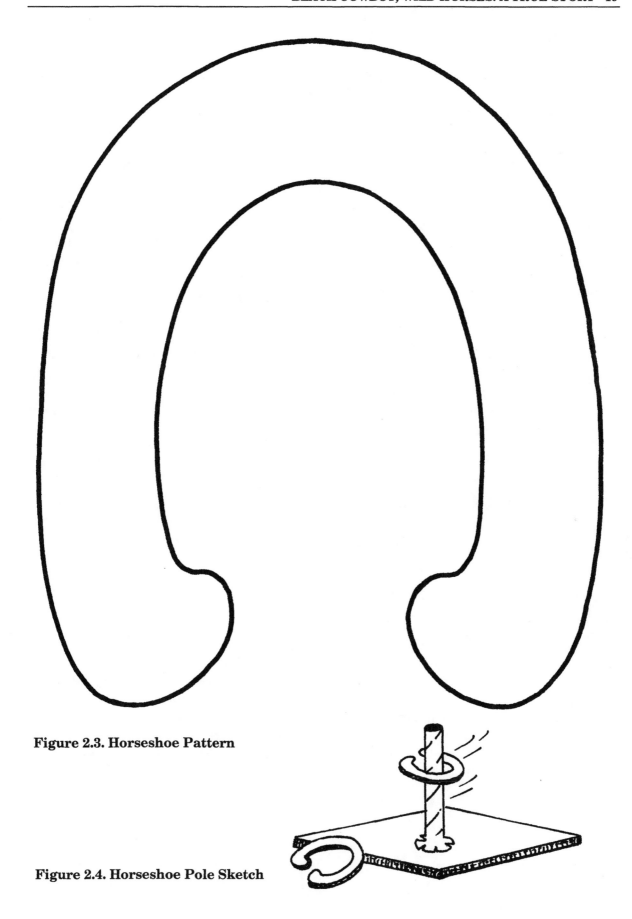

Figure 2.3. Horseshoe Pattern

Figure 2.4. Horseshoe Pole Sketch

The Game

Assuming that you have sixteen participants, make four playing areas. This will accommodate all sixteen players at one time. Each playing area consists of two horseshoe poles placed eight feet apart from each other. The children will stand next to one horseshoe pole and toss their horseshoes at the opposite horseshoe pole.

Each playing area will have four children, two teams of two individuals. One member from team A stands at one horseshoe pole, and his or her partner stands at the opposite horseshoe pole. The competing team, team B, also has members at each horseshoe pole.

The object of the game is for each child to toss two horseshoes at the opposite pole and score points. Starting at one end, decide who will go first. A member from team A tosses two horseshoes at the opposite pole. Then the person standing next to him from team B tosses two horseshoes at the opposite pole. The two team members standing at the opposite end count the points and record the score.

Then those two team members toss their horseshoes and their points are tallied. The horseshoe tossing moves back and forth, from one end to the other end, until one team wins. Usually the first team to score fifteen points is declared the winner. This number can be lowered to twelve or nine, if needed. At the end of a game, a team can challenge another team to a game or rechallenge the team they are playing against to another round.

Scoring

There are three ways to score points in the Tossing Horseshoes Game:

1. If the horseshoe encircles the pole, it is called a "ringer," and is worth three points.

2. If the horseshoe leans against the pole, it is called a "leaner," and is worth two points.

3. If the horseshoe lands close to the pole, it is worth one point. (To measure whether the shoe is close enough to the pole to earn points, take another horseshoe and stand one side next to the pole. The space from one leg of the horseshoe to the other leg, approximately four to five inches, is the area that can earn points. If the thrown horseshoe is within this area from the pole, it earns one point.) Children can take a horseshoe and measure for themselves after each throw, or a circle five inches from the pole can be drawn on the cardboard. Use a marker so that it is easily seen.

Craft

Create a Branded Kerchief Craft

Figure 2.5. Kerchief Sketch

✓ **SUPPLIES**

Muslin

Permanent markers (a variety of colors; 2 to 3 per student)

Paper and pencils

Making the Kerchief

Muslin is a plain, lightweight, and inexpensive material that can be located easily in most fabric stores. Cut the fabric into 21-by-21-inch squares. Give each child a fabric square and a couple of colored permanent markers. Remind them that permanent markers can stain their clothes, so they should be careful not to mark the clothes they are wearing.

Each child will create his or her own brand and then draw it on the muslin with the permanent markers. When finished, the children can fold the fabric into triangles and wear them around their necks as kerchiefs.

Normally, brands are very simple; they can be based on one's name or on something one likes a lot. See Figure 2.6, page 22, for examples.

Give the children pencils and pieces of paper on which to draw sample brands. Once a brand is decided upon, the child can use a permanent marker to draw the brand on one corner or all four corners of his or her kerchief.

So that the brand is visible when the muslin is worn around the neck, instruct the students to be sure and draw their brands in the corner(s) of their kerchiefs. Refer to the sample illustration above.

Figure 2.6. Cattle Brands

Snacks

Canned pinto beans (1 15-ounce can per four children)

Biscuits or rolls (1 per child)

Tea or apple cider (1 cup per child)

Canned peaches (1 15-ounce can per three children)

Slow cooker to keep beans warm (plus a serving spoon)

Aluminum pie tins (1 per child)

Coffee cups (1 per child)

Forks or spoons (1 per child)

A fun snack is warm beans (Texas cowboys called these "Pecos strawberries") and biscuits in aluminum pie tins. Keep beans warm in a slow cooker, and purchase rolls at a grocery store bakery. Serve warm tea or apple cider as a substitute for coffee.

On a cattle drive, the menu was routine and dull for cowhands. Usually they ate beans, biscuits, bacon, and coffee three times a day, unless they were lucky enough to catch a fish or trade for eggs with a farmer. Sometimes the camp cook served canned tomatoes or peaches for a break from the ordinary. Canned peaches can be served as a substitute for the beans and biscuits.

For atmosphere, stack several small tree logs together to create a fake campfire. Have the children sit on "bedrolls" (blankets) around the campfire eating their warm beans and biscuits.

Other Titles to Share

Antle, Nancy. *Sam's Wild West Show*. Illustrated by Simms Taback. New York: Dial Books for Young Readers, 1995. [40 pages]

Sam and his "Wild West Show" performers save a town from two bank robbers.

Applet, Kathi. *Cowboy Dreams*. Illustrated by Barry Root. New York: HarperCollins, 1999. [32 pages]

Rhyming, easy-to-read text tells of a young boy's nighttime dream of joining cowboys around the evening campfire.

Birney, Betty G. *Tyrannosaurus Tex*. Illustrated by John O'Brien. Boston: Houghton Mifflin, 1994. [32 pages]

Towering Tyrannosaurus Tex arrives at a cattle roundup in a 10,000-gallon hat. The cowhands are nervous until he saves the herd from cattle thieves.

Brimer, Larry Dane. *Cowboy Up!* Illustrated by Susan Miller. New York: Children's Press, 1999. [32 pages]

A rhyming beginning-to-read text about a young boy who rides a bucking bronco at the rodeo.

Gibbons, Gail. *Yippee-Yay! A Book About Cowboys and Cowgirls*. Little, Brown, 1998. [32 pages]

A factual book about cowhands and their work driving cattle from Texas to points north in Kansas, Missouri, Colorado, and Nebraska.

Harper, Jo. *Jalapeño Hal*. Illustrated by Jennifer Beck Harris. New York: Four Winds Press, 1993. [35 pages]

Jalapeño Hal is one tough hombre whose inventive use of hot peppers saves the town of Presidio.

Johnston, Tony. *Sparky and Eddie: Wild, Wild Rodeo!* Illustrated by Susannah Ryan. New York: Scholastic Press, 1998. [40 pages]

Sparky and Eddie participate in the school's unique rodeo contest. The ideas presented in this book would make a fun event for students in kindergarten through first grade.

Kellogg, Steven. *Pecos Bill*. New York: William Morrow, 1986. [42 pages]

Kellogg retells some of the stories surrounding America's most famous cowboy.

Ketteman, Helen. *Bubba the Cowboy Prince: A Fractured Texas Tale*. Illustrated by James Warhola. New York: Scholastic Press, 1997. [32 pages]

A cowboy Cinderella story in which Bubba, who has an evil stepdaddy and two lazy stepbrothers, meets the female rancher of his dreams at the ball.

Kimmel, Eric A. *Four Dollars and Fifty Cents*. Illustrated by Glen Rounds. New York: Holiday House, 1990. [32 pages]

To avoid paying his debt of four dollars and fifty cents, Short Long plays a trick on Widow Macrae and almost has his nose cut off by outlaws.

Knowlton, Laurie Lazzaro. *Why Cowboys Need a Brand*. Illustrated by James Rice. Gretna, LA: Pelican Publishing, 1996. [32 pages]

Slim Jim Watkins gains all the makings for his own ranch but cannot think of a brand.

———. *Why Cowboys Sleep with Their Boots On*. Illustrated by James Rice. Gretna, LA: Pelican Publishing, 1995. [32 pages]

Different animals steal Slim Jim Watkins's articles of clothing each night until he creates a solution.

Miller, Robert H. *The Story of Nat Love*. Illustrated by Michael Bryant. Morristown, NJ: Silver Press, 1995. [28 pages]

Nat Love was born a slave, but after the Civil War he leaves home and becomes the well-known cowboy by the name of Deadwood Dick.

Pinkney, Andrea Davis. *Bill Pickett, a Rodeo Ridin' Cowboy*. Illustrated by Brian Pinkney. New York: Harcourt Brace, 1996. [33 pages]

The true story of Bill Pickett, cowboy and rodeo star, and how he invents the bull-dogging method of subduing cattle.

Rice, James. *Prairie Night Before Christmas*. Gretna, LA: Pelican Publishing, 1986. [32 pages]

Two cowhands unknowingly help Santa Claus when his team of reindeer abandons him.

Sanfield, Steve. *The Great Turtle Drive*. Illustrated by Dirk Zimmer. New York: Alfred A. Knopf, 1996. [34 pages]

A cowboy collects 20,000 turtles and takes them on a five-year turtle drive from the plains of west Texas to Frenchy's Gourmet Eating Establishment and Pizza Parlor in Kansas City.

Stewart, Gail. *Mustangs and Wild Horses*. Photographs by William Muñoz. Minneapolis, MN: Capstone Press, 1996. [48 pages]

Tells the origin and history of mustangs and the controversial future for survival that they face today.

Contacting the Publisher

Contact the marketing department of Dial Books for Young Readers, Penguin Putnam, Inc., 375 Hudson Street, New York, NY 10014, 212-366-2800, http://www.penguinputnam.com. Ask what promotional items they have for *Black Cowboys, Wild Horses* such as posters, bookmarks, and the author's and illustrator's biographies. Request enough supplies for each child in your book club and your files.

CHAPTER 3

The Pumpkin Man from Piney Creek

By Darleen Bailey Beard

Illustrated by Laura Kelly

Beard, Darleen Bailey. *The Pumpkin Man from Piney Creek*. Illustrated by Laura Kelly. New York: Simon & Schuster Books for Young Readers, 1995. [32 pages]

Pa needs to sell each pumpkin he has grown, and cannot spare one for Hattie to make a jack-o'-lantern.

Introduction

The fall season brings much activity. School is in session, leaves are changing color, and the air is as crisp and fragrant as a McIntosh apple. People are shopping for the right pumpkin and planning their holiday costumes. *The Pumpkin Man from Piney Creek* is the perfect title to share September through November because of its theme and illustrations. During these months, children can sympathize with Hattie wanting to keep a pumpkin for her own jack-o'-lantern.

Serve snacks and distribute the Pumpkin Patch Drawing Page (Figure 3.2, page 33) as the children arrive. Once everyone has gathered, play Crayon Charades or the Pin the Face on the Pumpkin game. Follow with the introduction of the author and illustrator, and the discussion session. If time allows, end with the Autumn Leaf Rubbings craft. Before the children leave the room, show related titles for checkout and give the title for next week's book club.

Introducing the Author and Illustrator

Darleen Bailey Beard

Used by permission of Darleen Bailey Beard.

When Beard was a little girl she was not allowed to have a jack-o'-lantern, dress in a costume, or go trick-or-treating. She saw other kids in the neighborhood who had glowing pumpkins on their porches and thought they looked so beautiful.

"Hattie is me," says Beard. "I am that little girl who wants a jack-o'-lantern more than anything."

The idea for *Pumpkin Man from Piney Creek* came while Beard was researching the tradition of carving pumpkins into jack-o'-lanterns. The custom came to the United States with Irish immigrants during the mid-1800s. The immigrants had carved rutabagas and turnips in Ireland, but when they moved to the United States they discovered pumpkins, which were larger and easier to carve.

Beard says her two favorite illustrations in the book are Hattie sitting on the stoop and the last illustration in the book. "I like the one of Hattie sitting on the stoop hugging her knees. She is so disappointed about not having a pumpkin to carve," says Beard. "Behind her the door is painted blue—which is symbolic of how Hattie felt.

"Everybody has wanted something so badly that they were tempted to be dishonest to get it," says Beard. "Hattie hid that pumpkin from her dad because she wanted a jack-o'-lantern so badly. Then she does the right thing by giving the hidden pumpkin to the Pumpkin Man, and gets what she wants in the end—a jack-o'-lantern."

Beard used a replica of a 1902 Sears, Roebuck & Co. catalog for some of her research. She wanted the Pumpkin Man to be bigger than life; so Beard gave him a fine beaver hat and a wagon with a high-spring seat. "When I looked through the section on men's clothing, the beaver hats were the most expensive," says Beard. "And in the section on wagons, the most expensive wagons had the high-spring seats." Raspberry cream candies were also listed in the catalog.

Beard is the mother of two children, Spencer and Karalee, and is a full-time author. She was born on January 24, 1961 in Levittown, Pennsylvania, and graduated from the University of Oklahoma in 1986 with a B.A. in professional writing.

When she visits schools she always tells children to believe in themselves. "You have the power to make your dreams come true, and don't let people or what they say stand in your way."

Address correspondence to Darleen Bailey Beard at 1627 Briarcliff Court, Norman, OK 73071.

Laura Kelly

Used by permission of Laura Kelly.

Kelly dedicated her artwork in *The Pumpkin Man From Piney Creek* to her grandparents Sally S. Harris and George W. Harris. "My grandmother has been very encouraging to my work. She's been a cheerleader," says Kelly. This encouragement has, to date, led Kelly to illustrate eight children's books. "I knew I wanted to be an artist all my life. I always had a direction and goal in art. I never had to struggle with what I wanted to be," said Kelly.

When asked which illustration in the book is her favorite, Kelly says it is the one of Hattie, the old woman, and the man with the pig looking through the J. Horn Feed & Seed window. The old woman is Tasha Tudor, a children's books illustrator. Kelly admires Tudor's artwork and collects books by and about her. The other people were modeled on neighbors who once lived on her street.

Kelly is married to James, an industrial designer, and has two boys: Connor and Graeme. They live in the mountains outside of Los Angeles, California.

Kelly was born in Los Angeles on January 26, 1958, and studied art at California State University, Long Beach. Both she and James won scholarships to attend and met at the awards ceremony.

When speaking to children Kelly stresses, "Art is not a magical gift. It comes about by practicing. If you do it enough, and like it enough, you can be good. Don't be discouraged if you're not good in the beginning. You can learn to be an artist. Keep a sketchbook and draw every day."

You may write to Laura Kelly c/o Simon & Schuster Books for Young Readers, 1230 Avenue of the Americas, New York, NY 10022.

Discussion Questions

Make sixteen photocopies of the pumpkin graphic (Figure 3.1, page 31) on orange construction paper. Reproduce the questions (page 32) on white bond paper. Cut and glue them to the back of the pumpkin graphics. Laminate, if possible, and cut along the outlines of the pumpkins.

Pass the discussion questions around in a small basket. The pumpkins should be face up with the questions hidden from view. Have one child select a pumpkin from the basket, read the question aloud, and give his or her opinion or answer. If desired, the discussion can be opened to the group for others to give their viewpoints or thoughts. Then the child passes the basket to the next individual who repeats the process. Allow only one pumpkin to be drawn at a time. This prevents others from reading and concentrating on their questions and not listening to what is being discussed.

Remember, some of the discussion questions have more than one answer, or there is no "right" answer. Children may voice a completely different response than expected.

Activities

Pumpkin Patch Drawing Page

Reproduce Figure 3.2 (page 33) for each child. Pass out crayons or colored pencils. Tell the children to imagine themselves in their own pumpkin field and draw what they would see.

Figure 3.1. Pumpkin for Discussion Questions

Discussion Questions

What would it be like to be a farmer?	Why did Hattie hide the pumpkin when she was helping Pa?
How did Hattie feel when she gave the Pumpkin Man her pumpkin?	The author dedicated her book to her fifth-grade teacher. To whom would you dedicate your book?
What kind of face do you like on your jack-o'-lantern?	What is your favorite pie?
Which picture in the book is your favorite?	What do you wish for?
What were the two things the Pumpkin Man gave to Hattie?	Describe Hattie.
Why did the Pumpkin Man give Hattie the pumpkin?	Why was Pa going to give Ma's pumpkin to the Pumpkin Man?
What are some of the animals shown in the illustrations?	What do you like best about this story?
How do you know it is the fall season? What clues does the illustrator use?	Hattie's nickname was Hattie-Pattie. Do you have a favorite nickname?

Pumpkin Patch Drawing Page

What would your pumpkin field look like? Would you have big pumpkins or little pumpkins? And how about a scarecrow, rake, and wheelbarrow? Draw a picture of your pumpkin patch.

Figure 3.2. Pumpkin Patch Drawing Page

Crayon Charades Game

✓ **SUPPLIES**

Flip chart with paper (may substitute with a chalkboard and call
    the game "Chalkboard Charades")

Crayons

One small basket, or some other type of container

Scrap typing paper

Pencil

Preparation

Using a pencil, write the numbers one through sixteen (or whatever the
number of players is) on small slips of folded paper. Before starting the game, each
participant will draw a piece of paper to determine the order of play. Start with
the child who draws number sixteen and work backwards: player fourteen, thirteen, twelve, and so forth.

Create another set of small slips of folded paper. Write the objects that the
players will draw. See below for suggested subjects to sketch.

The Game

Each participant will take a turn at the drawing board. The player will
select a folded slip of paper from the basket. On the paper is written the object to
be drawn, and the group tries to guess what the player is portraying. For example,
if the player takes a slip of paper that reads "horse," he or she will begin to draw a
horse while the group guesses what the object is. As soon as a drawing is correctly
identified, the drawer joins the group and the next player steps up to the drawing
board.

All suggested subjects for the game come from either *The Pumpkin Man
from Piney Creek* or from the fall season. The group should keep this in mind as
they guess.

Suggested Subjects for Crayon Charades

Leaf, turkey, cow, horse, chicken, pig, barn, Ma's blue-ribbon pie, Hattie,
Pa, Pumpkin Man's hat, jack-o'-lantern, wagonload of pumpkins, corn bread and
beans, sunflower, basket, pile of hay, pumpkin field, Pa's money (six bills), coffee
cup, and cat.

Pin the Face on the Pumpkin Game

✓ **SUPPLIES**

Orange heavyweight poster board

Black lightweight poster board or construction paper

Adhesive tape

Blindfold

Preparation

Draw and cut out a large pumpkin from orange poster board and tape it to the wall. Use Figure 3.1 (page 31) as a pattern. Enlarge Figure 3.1 on a photocopier or place on an opaque projector and trace the pumpkin outline onto the poster board. If possible, laminate the pumpkin so that it can be used again in the future.

Cut different shaped eyes, noses, and mouths from the black construction paper. Again, laminate them to prevent wear and tear. Refer to Figure 3.3 (page 36) for a sampling of jack-o'-lantern facial features.

The Game

This game is based on the well-loved party game, Pin the Tail on the Donkey. Place a piece, or several pieces, of adhesive tape on each face part. Place the blindfold on the first player and gently spin the child around two times. Point the child in the general direction of the pumpkin face. The child walks to the pumpkin and sticks the eye, nose, or mouth onto the pumpkin.

Have each child select a different facial part until you have built a jack-o'-lantern. Be sure to stress that the children cannot feel the pumpkin to see where they should place their parts. They just need to stick the part wherever their hands land.

Everyone will giggle at the comical jack-o'-lanterns they produce. Once a face is completed, remove the parts and start again.

EYES

NOSES

MOUTHS

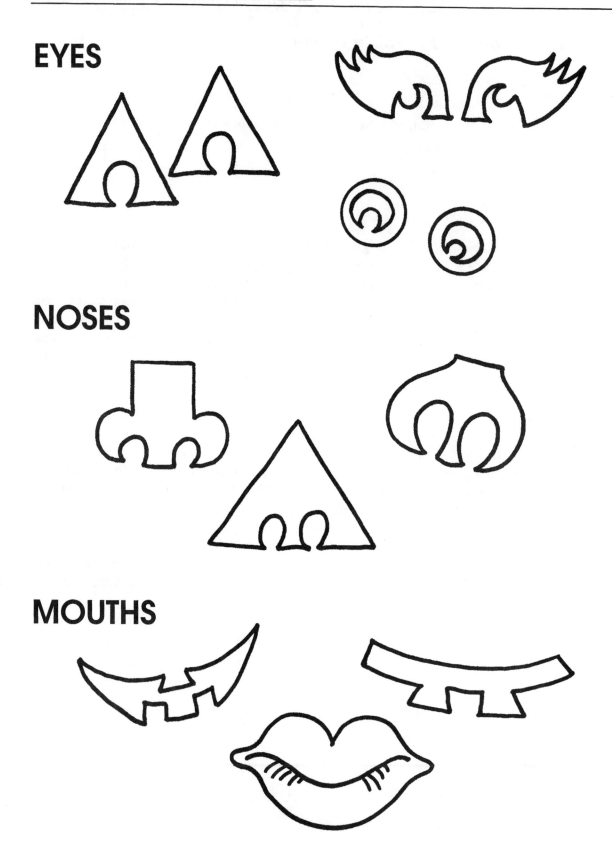

Figure 3.3. Jack-o'-Lantern Facial Features

Craft

Autumn Leaf Rubbings Craft

✓ **SUPPLIES**

Leaves

White bond paper

Crayons

Leaf identification book (optional)

Magnifying glasses (optional)

Before the program, collect a variety of leaves. Gather enough so children have several shapes and sizes from which to choose. The leaves cannot be too dry or they will crumble when the children color over them.

Leaf rubbings are easy to make and can be very vibrant using fall colors such as reds, oranges, yellows, and browns. However, any color will make for a bright and unique creation. Old crayons work best because the paper covering can be removed and the children can use the side of the crayon, not the tip. If possible, use the wide crayons because they are easier to grip.

Place a leaf under the white paper. Rub the crayon across the paper, above the leaf, until the shape and texture of the leaf are visible. Keep coloring different leaves until the paper is full or until the child has completed his or her master-piece. Make your own leaf rubbing to demonstrate the process so the group has clear instructions on how to do it.

At the end of the session have the children show their leaf rubbings and share what they like best about the fall season; for example, "What I like best about fall is raking leaves with my mom," or "What I like best about fall is eating pumpkin pie."

Another option to this craft is to make simple leaf identification books and magnifying glasses available. Help children discover from which trees their leaves came.

Snacks

Pumpkin-shaped sugar cookies (recipe below)

Orange juice

Serve pumpkin-shaped sugar cookies with orange frosting or orange-colored sprinkles. Sugar cookies are easy to make, or you can buy the premade dough in the grocery store. Purchase or borrow a pumpkin-shaped cookie cutter to create the shape. Prepare orange juice to drink.

Sugar Cookie Recipe

INGREDIENTS _____

⅔ cup shortening
¾ cup sugar
1 egg
½ tsp. vanilla

4 tsp. milk
2 cups flour
½ tsp. salt
1 tsp. baking powder

DIRECTIONS

Set oven at 375°. Cream shortening until fluffy. Beat in sugar. Add egg and vanilla. Stir well and add milk. In a separate bowl sift together flour, salt, and baking powder. Add the flour mixture to the shortening mixture and stir well. Cover the bowl with plastic wrap and chill for one hour in the refrigerator. Remove and roll out on a lightly floured surface to a ⅛-inch thickness. Lightly flour pumpkin-shaped cutter and cut shapes into dough. Place on a lightly greased cookie sheet one-inch apart. Bake for 6 to 8 minutes. Makes two dozen.

Other Titles to Share

Arnold, Marsha Diane. *The Pumpkin Runner*. Illustrated by Brad Sneed. New York: Dial Books for Young Readers, 1998. [32 pages]

Sheep rancher Joshua Summerhayes and Yellow Dog run in the twelfth Annual Koala-K Race—fueled by pumpkin power.

Dillon, Jana. *Jeb Scarecrow's Pumpkin Patch*. Boston: Houghton Mifflin, 1992. [32 pages]

Jeb must find a way to keep the crows from holding their annual celebration in his pumpkin patch.

Fowler, Allan. *How Do You Know It's Fall?* Chicago: Childrens Press, 1992. [32 pages]

Discusses the different signs of the fall season such as squirrels gathering nuts and farmers harvesting their crops.

Hirschi, Ron. *Fall*. Photographs by Thomas D. Mangelsen. New York: Cobblehill Books, 1991. [32 pages]

A beautifully written, spare description of what happens in the natural world as the fall season arrives and then links with winter.

Markle, Sandra. *Exploring Autumn: A Season of Science Activities, Puzzlers, and Games.* New York: Atheneum, 1991. [152 pages]

A unique collection of information and activities related to the fall season. Contains information about the fall season, plants, animals, pilgrims, Halloween, Columbus Day, and the election of a United States president.

Robbins, Ken. *Autumn Leaves*. New York: Scholastic Press, 1998. [40 pages]

Robbins, a photographer, illustrates a simple and beautiful book identifying the leaves of thirteen trees.

Sloat, Teri. *Patty's Pumpkin Patch*. New York: G. P. Putnam's Sons, 1999. [32 pages]

A rhyming text tells about the life of a pumpkin patch from seed to sale. Following the story is an A to Z of animals, birds, and insects found within the pumpkin field.

White, Linda. *Too Many Pumpkins*. Illustrated by Megan Lloyd. New York: Holiday House, 1996. [32 pages]

By accident, pumpkins begin to grow in Rebecca Estelle's yard. Problem is, Rebecca hates pumpkins.

Yacowitz, Caryn. *Pumpkin Fiesta*. Illustrated by Joe Capeda. New York: HarperCollins, 1998. [32 pages]

Foolish Fernando tries to copy Old Juana's method for growing winning pumpkins. Old Juana's recipe for pumpkin soup in a pumpkin is included.

Zagwyn, Deborah Turney. *The Pumpkin Blanket*. Berkeley, CA: Tricycle Press, 1995. [32 pages]

Clee must decide whether or not she wants to sacrifice her beautiful blanket to save her family's pumpkin patch.

Zolotow, Charlotte. *Say It!* Illustrated by James Stevenson. New York: Greenwillow Books, 1980. [25 pages]

A mother and her young daughter take a walk in the late afternoon of a windy fall day.

Contacting the Publisher

Contact the marketing department for Simon & Schuster at 1230 Avenue of the Americas, New York, NY 10022, 212-698-7200, http://www.simonsays.com. Ask what promotional items they have for *The Pumpkin Man from Piney Creek*, such as posters, bookmarks, and the author's and illustrator's biographies. Request enough for supplies for each child in your book club and your files.

CHAPTER 4

Commander Toad and the Space Pirates

By Jane Yolen
Illustrated by Bruce Degen

Yolen, Jane. *Commander Toad and the Space Pirates.* Illustrated by Bruce Degen. New York: Penguin Putnam Books for Young Readers, 1997. [64 pages]

Commander Toad and his crew have read all the books, viewed all the videos, and played all the games that are aboard Star Warts. They are bored until space pirates attack their ship.

Introduction

Humans have always possessed the desire to see what they have not seen, to explore new frontiers. Two hundred years ago, President Thomas Jefferson sent U.S. Army officers Meriwether Lewis and William Clark to explore and report on the little-known territory west of the Mississippi River. The United States had acquired vast tracts of land through the Louisiana Purchase, and President Jefferson hoped that the explorers would make contact with the people living in this region, record the plant and animal life, and trace the boundaries of the Purchase.

Today, space is the remaining unexplored frontier, and its boundaries appear endless. As scientists study the universe with their telescopes and unmanned space probes, we learn more about our solar system and beyond.

More than twenty years ago, engineers, scientists, and technicians from the National Aeronautics and Space Administration and the Jet Propulsion Laboratory designed and built two unmanned spacecraft, Voyager 1 and Voyager 2, to probe the hostile environment of deep space. Launched in 1977, they are still exploring the universe. Voyagers 1 and 2 were built to collect scientific data until 2020 (http://vraptor.hpl.nasa.gov/voyager/voyager.html). Through the Voyagers' cameras, radio antennas, plasma wave detectors, ultrviolet spectrometers and magnetometers, we have seen our distant planets and their moons.

One of Saturn's nine moons, named Phoebe, has a retrograde orbit. In other words, it travels in the opposite direction of Saturn's orbiting spin. Triton, Neptune's largest moon, also travels backward. Even though no humans have yet traveled beyond Earth's moon, many children dream of boarding a spaceship and voyaging to distant galaxies.

Jane Yolen and Bruce Degen have collaborated on a series of books that provide humorous and exciting adventures into space. Commander Toad and his crew not only encounter pirates in their exploration of "deep, dark space," but giant grapes, a Deep Wader, intergalactic spies, and strange toad-um poles.

In *Commander Toad and the Space Pirates*, boredom and repetition have dulled the crew until a spacecraft bearing the skull and crossbones traps them. Throughout the text, Yolen uses puns and alliterations to delight her readers, and Degen jumps on board using tongue-in-cheek, humorous illustrations.

Begin the session by serving snacks and presenting either the Constellation Connect-the-Dots (Figure 4.2, page 48) or A Spacey Word Scramble (Figure 4.3, page 50) activity sheet as the children arrive. Once everyone has gathered, proceed with information about the author and illustrator followed by the discussion session. If the moderator opts to create the Papier-Mâché Space Pirate (pages 51–53), and this is highly recommended, it will take two sessions to complete the craft. During the second session, have the children paint their pirates. While the heads are drying, read another title from the Commander Toad series or one of Daniel Pinkwater's amusing *Fat Men from Space* or *Guys from Space* (see "Other Titles to Share" in this chapter).

An alternative to the Papier-Mâché Space Pirate craft is to play the Space Mummy Game or make a Toadly Cool Spaceship.

Introducing the Author and Illustrator

Jane Yolen

Photo by Shulamith Oppenheim. Used by permission from Penguin Putnam Books for Young Readers.

Jane Yolen writes the series of Commander Toad books because she loves puns and science fiction adventures.

Commander Toad is based in part on her son Adam. When Adam was very young he used to be scared to go upstairs to bed because he was afraid of the long, dark hallway in their home. Yolen addressed Adam's fear in her very first Commander Toad book, *Commander Toad in Space*, by writing, "You cannot be brave unless you are first very much afraid."

Commander Toad and the Space Pirates is a combination of two interests: science fiction and pirates. In addition to being a writer and a reader of science fiction (Ursula Le Guin is her favorite science fiction author), stories about pirates have always charmed Yolen. Her first published book was *Pirates in Petticoats* (McKay, 1963), and one of the very first books she wrote, while an eighth grader at Hunter Junior High School, was a short, nonfiction piece about pirates.

"I was mostly fascinated by women pirates," says Yolen. "There had been a chapter [about them] in my junior high book. I also did a picture book, years later, called *The Ballad of the Pirate Queens* (Harcourt Brace, 1995)."

Yolen is a prolific author, writing for adults, young adults, and children. Not only does she compose stories about toads, frogs, and pirates, but she writes literary folk and fairy tales, adult and juvenile novels and nonfiction, and poetry, such as *Snow, Snow: Winter Poems for Children* (illustrated by son Jason Stemple; Boyd Mills, 1998) and *Bird Watch: A Book of Poetry* (Penguin Putnam, 1999).

To date, Yolen and Degen have collaborated on seven Commander Toad books. Yolen first met Bruce Degen at a book signing following the publication of *Commander Toad in Space*. "We had a riotous signing at ALA (American Library Association conference), trying to one-up one another in writing punny autographs," says Yolen. Currently, Yolen is working on a new adventure titled, *Commander Toad and the Lizard of Ooze*.

Yolen is married to David Stemple and has three grown children: Heidi Elisabet, Adam Douglas, and Jason Fredric, and three granddaughters. She was born February 11, 1939 in New York City and earned a B.A. from Smith College, and master of education from the University of Massachusetts. She and her husband make their homes in Massachusetts and St. Andrews, Scotland.

Write to Jane Yolen at Phoenix Farm, 31 School Street, Box 27, Hatfield, MA 01038, or visit her Web site at http://www.janeyolen.com. The Web site includes links to more biographical information, plus a section containing lesson plans and suggested activities for teachers.

Bruce Degen

Used by permission from Penguin Putnam
Books for Young Readers.

B ruce Degen must draw in his sleep. He is the illustrator of six of his own titles and the illustrator of over seventy titles for other authors. In addition to Jane Yolen's Commander Toad series, he is also the well-respected illustrator of Joanna Cole's The Magic School Bus series.

Refna Wilkin, a now-retired editor for Putnam, asked Degen to illustrate the Commander Toad books. "The editors or art directors, who always match the artist up with the authors, are the unsung heroes of children's books," says Degen. "It was quite a gift to me, a fairly new book illustrator to be paired with such a well-known and prestigious author, Jane Yolen.

"Working on a text by Jane Yolen is always a delight. She writes so well, and these books are funny! I love that each book is usually full of puns, real groaners. And actually the major idea for each book is based on a major pun. She is so hip to all the *Star Trek*, *Star Wars*, sci-fi things that kids just love to catch the references in the Commander Toad books."

Degen illustrates the series using pencil and watercolor. *Commander Toad and the Voyage Home* is the only one, to date, in full color. He says, "In the bad old days of printing, before the laser scanner, only limited color was affordable in many children's books. Then the artist had to separate the layers of color himself into different sheets for each color. That is why Sendak's Little Bear series, and Lobel's Frog and Toad books are only black with two colors. Commander Toad books are all black, green, and red. The brown comes from overlapping green and red. Only *Commander Toad and the Planet of the Grapes* is different—it is green and purple, for the purple grapes."

As a child, Degen drew all the time and was always interested in art. A relative owned a small printing shop and Degen would get odd trimmings of paper to use. On Saturdays he sometimes attended classes at the Brooklyn Museum. The group would sketch in the gallery and on warm weather days visit the botanical gardens next door.

"I went to a special high school in New York City for art, even though the subway trip was almost an hour and a half each way from my house, and got a B.F.A. in art from The Cooper Union and an M.F.A. from the Pratt Institute in printmaking and painting.

"I feel very blessed to be able to work on children's books. The illustration is fun to do and I actually get paid to do exactly what I like. I also write books, and then illustrate them. Some of the kids may have read *Jamberry* (HarperCollins, 1998), *Sailaway Home* (Scholastic, 1996), and *The Little Witch and the Riddle* (Harper & Row, 1980). But I am a slow writer and a fast drawer, so there is a lot of time between my books. The latest is *Daddy Is a Doodlebug* (HarperCollins, 2000)."

Degen was born June 14, 1945 in Brooklyn, New York. He is married to Christine Bostard, a teacher and illustrator. They have two grown sons, Benjamin and Alexander. They too are artists. A chocolate Labrador named Bailey completes the family portrait.

When visiting schools, Degen tells children that if they want something, they need to persevere and work hard. "I am illustrating books because I decided I really, really liked it and had to do it. I went out with my portfolio and tried lots of ideas, and something clicked. It didn't happen right away, but it would never have happened if I weren't completely convinced that I had to make it happen by sticking with it and not taking no for an answer. And working hard at it too.

"The world is filled with talented people, but only some really devote themselves, and they are the ones who have success in their work. So if you like to draw, or write, do it, do it, do it! Do it for your own pleasure, not just because a teacher asks you to. Who knows, if you stick with it you will find the thing that works for you."

Address correspondence to Bruce Degen c/o Penguin Putnam, Inc., 375 Hudson Street, New York, NY 10014.

Discussion Questions

Make sixteen photocopies of Figure 4.1 (page 46) on white paper and color them. Reproduce the questions (page 47) on white bond paper. Cut and glue them to the back of the graphics. Laminate, if possible, and cut along the outlines of the spaceships.

Pass the discussion questions around in a small basket. The spaceships should be face up with the questions hidden from view. Have one child select a spaceship from the basket, read the question aloud, and give his or her opinion or answer. If desired, the discussion can be opened to the group for others to give their viewpoints or thoughts. Then the child passes the basket to the next individual who repeats the process. Allow only one spaceship to be drawn at a time. This prevents others from reading and concentrating on their questions and not listening to what is being discussed.

Remember, some of the discussion questions have more than one answer, or there is no "right" answer. Children may voice a completely different response than expected.

Activities

Constellation Connect-the-Dots

Photocopy the activity sheet (Figure 4.2, page 48) for each child in the book club.

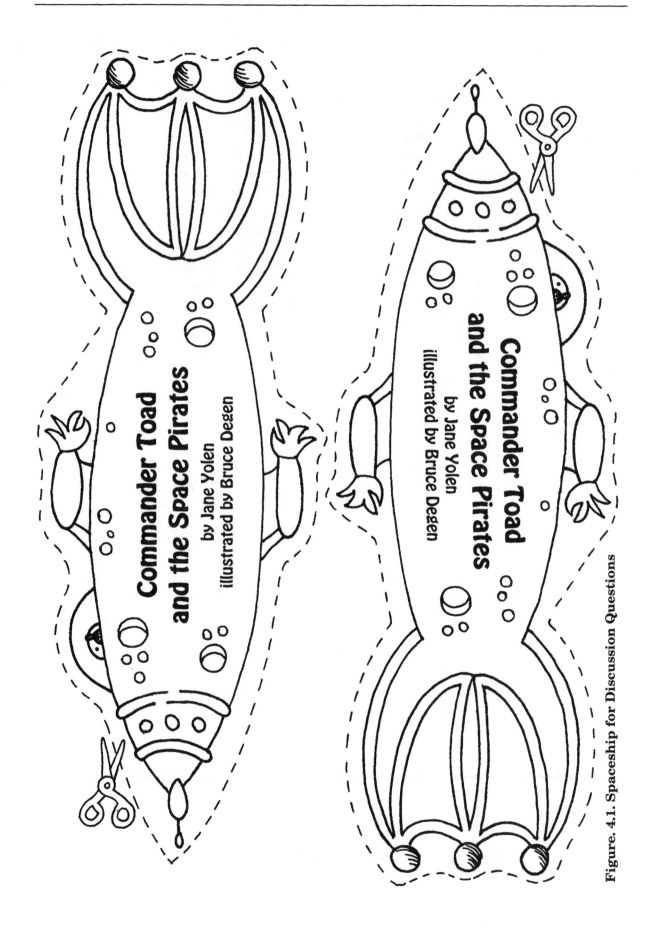

Figure. 4.1. Spaceship for Discussion Questions

Discussion Questions

What would you do if Commander Toad landed in your backyard?	What did you like or dislike about the space pirates?
Tell the group what the story is about.	How did the space pirates capture Commander Toad's ship?
What job would you want on a spaceship?	Share your favorite illustration. Tell why you like it.
Which planet would you visit and why?	What color is Commander Toad's spaceship?
Name the members of Commander Toad's crew.	If you discovered a planet, what would you name it?
How were the pirates bad?	What games do you play when you are bored?
What do you like best about this book?	How was Commander Toad's crew saved from the pirates?
Commander Salamander is also called what other names?	Which *Star Warts* crew member do you want to be?

Figure 4.2. Contellation Connect-the-Dots

A Spacey Word Scramble Activity Sheet

Photocopy the following activity sheet (Figure 4.3, page 50) for each child in the book club. Answers to the activity are below.

A Spacey Word Scramble Answer Key

1.	TOAD	9.	SALAMANDER
2.	LILY	10.	BOOKS
3.	SPACE	11.	VIDEOS
4.	PLANK	12.	PEEPER
5.	PIRATES	13.	SKYJUMPER
6.	SHIP	14.	LUKE
7.	GOON	15.	MUMMY
8.	COMMANDER		

Space Mummy Game

✓ **SUPPLIES**

Two rolls of toilet paper per child

Three sheets of white tissue paper per child

Scraps of ribbon and/or yarn (12 to 14 inches in length)

10-inch length of foil per child

Adhesive tape

Kitchen timer

Stickers, pencils, bookmarks, or treats for prizes (one per child)

Divide the group into teams of two children per team. Give each team two rolls of toilet paper, three sheets of white tissue paper, a sheet of foil, four to ten lengths of scrap ribbon and/or yarn, and a roll of adhesive tape. The adult moderator tells each team they have five minutes to make one team member into a space mummy using some or all of the items given to them.

Set the timer for five minutes and tell the group "go!" At the end of the five minutes have the mummies go to the front of the room so that everyone can see their costumes. Give prizes, such as a pencils, bookmarks, or candies, as the adult moderator decides which team has won for: the scariest mummy, the silliest, the most unusual, the messiest, the most likely to fall apart in two minutes, the most likely to stay together for 100 years, the most colorful, the toadly coolest, the most toadly awesome, the mummiest looking, and so forth.

Have everyone clap for the space mummies. Then ask the children to return to their original teams. Refresh the supplies and repeat the process for the team members who have not yet been made into mummies. The current mummies can either keep their costumes on or tear them off before decorating their teammates.

A Spacey Word Scramble

Below are words from Jane Yolen's book *Commander Toad and the Space Pirates*. See how many you can unscramble. Write the correct word on the lines next to the scrambled word. For example, N P L A K would be written <u>P</u> <u>L</u> <u>A</u> <u>N</u> <u>K</u>, as in "walk the plank."

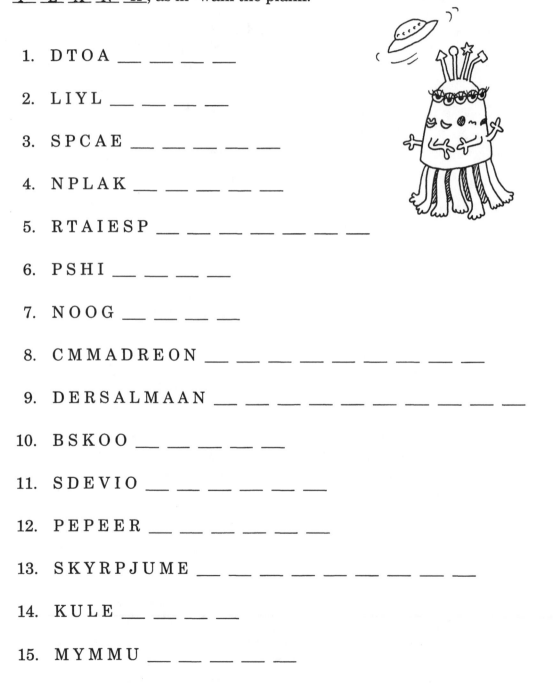

1. D T O A __ __ __ __

2. L I Y L __ __ __ __

3. S P C A E __ __ __ __ __

4. N P L A K __ __ __ __ __

5. R T A I E S P __ __ __ __ __ __ __

6. P S H I __ __ __ __

7. N O O G __ __ __ __

8. C M M A D R E O N __ __ __ __ __ __ __ __ __

9. D E R S A L M A A N __ __ __ __ __ __ __ __ __

10. B S K O O __ __ __ __ __

11. S D E V I O __ __ __ __ __ __

12. P E P E E R __ __ __ __ __ __

13. S K Y R P J U M E __ __ __ __ __ __ __ __ __

14. K U L E __ __ __ __

15. M Y M M U __ __ __ __ __

Figure 4.3. A Spacey Word Scramble

Crafts

Papier-Mâché Space Pirates Craft

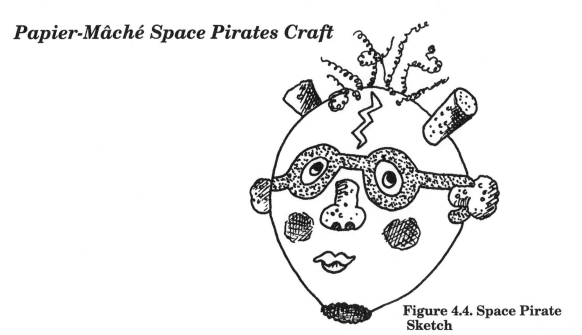

Figure 4.4. Space Pirate Sketch

✓ **SUPPLIES**

Newspaper cut into 1½-inch-wide strips

Papier-mâché paste (see recipe)

1 large balloon per child

Masking tape

Cool glue gun (adult use only)

Tempera paints of various colors

Paint brushes

Water

Paper towels for cleanup

2 or 3 corks per child (Paper towel or toilet paper tubes may be substituted.)

Scissors

1 bowl or pie tin per child

Wax paper

This is a wonderful craft. Do not let the "mess" involved with a papier-mâché project discourage you from presenting this activity to the children. Young people enjoy being able to use their hands and imaginations.

To create less work in cleaning up, cover all the tables and floor area with newspaper. When the students are finished, simply gather up the newspaper and throw it away—a clean room with little hassle. (If the room is carpeted, lay down extra layers of newspaper or plastic sheeting on the floor.)

To create facial features, gather wine or champagne corks. Ask for donations from friends, family, and colleagues. Champagne corks make good antennas, noses, or ears because of their mushroom shape. Instead of corks, one can also use paper towel or toilet paper tubes cut into two- or three-inch sections.

As mentioned earlier, this craft takes two sessions to complete. During the first session, the children will take the inflated balloons and create their papier-mâché pirate heads. At the second session, the children will paint their pirate heads.

Session 1

Following is the papier-mâché paste recipe and directions for creating the head. This recipe should make enough paste for three children to use. Multiply recipe for the number of children in your session.

The papier-mâché paste can be stored in the refrigerator for a couple of days. Just allow it to return to room temperature before the children use it.

Papier-Mâché Paste Recipe

INGREDIENTS

¼ cup flour
1 cup warm water
5 cups boiling water

DIRECTIONS

Mix one cup of warm water into flour slowly. Stir as you add the water. Consistency should be thin and runny. Pour this mixture into five cups of water boiling on the stove. Place on medium temperature and stir occasionally. When the mixture has begun to boil again, allow it to boil for three minutes. Cool to room temperature.

Pour paste into individual plastic bowls or larger bowls that can be shared between two individuals.

Note: Papier-mâché paste, such as Ross Art Paste or Art Paste (cellulose) is available for purchase at art and hobby stores.

> *Making Pirate Heads:*

Cut strips of newspaper 1½ inches wide and 12 inches long. Each child will need approximately five half-sheets of newspaper to complete a head. The students will dip the newspaper strips into the papier-mâché paste and squeegee away excess paste by pinching between their thumbs and index fingers.

Place three layers of newspaper on the balloon. Tell the children to dip the strips of newspaper into the paste and completely cover the balloon one time. Then tell them to cover the balloon two more times with paste and paper.

Allow the heads to dry for twenty-four to forty-eight hours. Place the heads on wax paper to dry and store on a table or counter that receives air circulation and light.

Session 2

Start the second session by asking the children to paint their space pirate heads following the directions below. While the heads are drying, read to the group *Fat Men from Space* by Daniel Pinkwater or one of the other Commander Toad books by Jane Yolen. Another option would be to booktalk other titles, such as those listed in "Other Titles to Share." Children may want to check these titles out at the end of the session to read at home.

Depending upon the situation, children may leave with their space pirate heads (place on a sheet of wax paper), or return later to retrieve them.

➢ *Painting Pirate Heads*

Again, for easy cleanup, cover the tables and floor with newspaper.

Tape or glue (using a crafter's cool glue gun) any corks or paper towel tubbing into place to make eyes, ears, noses, or antennas. Use tempera paints and several size brushes to paint the space pirate faces.

Toadly Cool Flying Spaceships Craft

Blocksma, Mary, and Dewey Blocksma. *Easy to Make Spaceships That Really Fly*. Englewood, NJ: Prentice Hall, 1985. [40 pages]

At this writing, the book is out of print, but interlibrary loan services at your public library may be able to help you obtain a copy of it. *Easy to Make Spaceships That Really Fly* contains easy patterns for spaceships using paper plates, paper cups and straws. They really do fly and are fun to make.

Snacks

Freeze-dried space food

Dried fruit

Powdered fruit drinks, such as lemonade or orange-flavored
beverages

Discuss with the book club members that astronauts travel with freeze-dried food. Dried fruit such as raisins and powdered drinks will give them an idea of what astronauts eat.

Although more expensive, space food can also be ordered from the Kennedy Space Center Visitor Complex by calling 800-621-9826 or visiting their Web site at http://www.thespaceshop.com.

The LuvyDuvy Corporation also sells freeze-dried ice cream, ice-cream sandwiches, and freeze-dried strawberries. The company advertises that their products were originally developed for the early Apollo missions and are manufactured by the same company that supplies freeze-dried foods to NASA and the space shuttle missions. Contact information is: LuvyDuvy Corporation, 1946 NW 54th Avenue, Margate, FL 33063, http://www.luvyduvy.com.

Other Titles to Share

Cazet, Denys. *Minnie and Moo Save the Earth*. New York: DK, 1999. [48 pages]

Two cows in a farmer's hot tub mistake an alien invasion as only comets falling to Earth.

Gaffney, Timothy. *Grandpa Takes Me to the Moon*. Illustrated by Barry Root. New York: Tambourine Books, 1996. [32 pages]

A young boy's astronaut grandfather tells about his trip to outer space and his walk on the moon.

Getz, David. *Floating Home*. Illustrated by Michael Rex. New York: Henry Holt, 1997. [36 pages]

Eight-year-old Maxine rides the space shuttle for a new perspective of home. During her trip she describes what astronauts wear and how they feel during takeoff.

Hatchett, Clint. *The Glow-in-the-Dark Night Sky Book*. Illustrated by Stephen Marchesi. New York: Random House, 1988. [20 pages]

Use the book's star maps and your own flashlight to locate constellations in the night sky.

MacDonald, Suse. *Space Spinners*. New York: Dial Books for Young Readers, 1991. [32 pages]

Reluctantly, Arabella joins her bold sister Kate as the first spiders to spin a web in space.

Pinkwater, Daniel. *Guys From Space*. New York: Macmillan, 1989. [32 pages]

Four guys from space arrive in a young boy's backyard and take him on a short, but adventurous, ride.

———. *Mush, a Dog from Space*. New York: Atheneum Books for Young Readers, 1995. [40 pages]

Kelly's parents will not allow her to have a dog until they meet Mush, the mushamute from space.

Yolen, Jane. *The Ballad of the Pirate Queens*. Illustrated by David Shannon. San Diego: Harcourt Brace, 1995. [32 pages]

Poetic verse tells of Anne Bonney and Mary Reade, two women pirates captured by Captain Barnet in 1720.

——. *Commander Toad and the Big Black Hole*. Illustrated by Bruce Degen. New York: Penguin Putnam Books for Young Readers, 1996. [64 pages]

The crew teaches a large mouth not to sing with its mouth full.

——. *Commander Toad and the Dis-Asteroid*. Illustrated by Bruce Degen. New York: Penguin Putnam Books for Young Readers, 1996. [64 pages]

Commander Toad and his crew must save inhabitants of an asteroid who are in trouble.

——. *Commander Toad and the Intergalactic Spy*. Illustrated by Bruce Degen. New York: Penguin Putnam Books for Young Readers, 1997. [64 pages]

Commander Toad must identify his cousin, Space Fleet's greatest spy Agent 007½, among other disguised and dangerous spies.

——. *Commander Toad and the Planet of the Grapes*. Illustrated by Bruce Degen. New York: Penguin Putnam Books for Young Readers, 1996. [64 pages]

The crew explores a new planet with initial, unseen dangers.

——. *Commander Toad and the Voyage Home*. Illustrated by Bruce Degen. New York: Penguin Putnam Books for Young Readers, 1998. [64 pages]

Commander Toad and his crew want to go HOME, but end up with an unexpected destination.

——. *Commander Toad in Space*. Illustrated by Bruce Degen. New York: Penguin Putnam Books for Young Readers, 1996. [64 pages]

In the first in the series of Commander Toad books, the crew land on a brand-new world and are forced to use their ingenuity to escape the Deep Wader.

Contacting the Publisher

Contact the marketing department at Penguin Putnam Inc., 375 Hudson Street, New York, NY 10014, 212-366-2000, http://www.penguinputnam.com. Ask what promotional items they have for *Commander Toad and the Space Pirates*, such as posters, bookmarks, and the author's and illustrator's biographies. Request enough supplies for each child in your book club and your files.

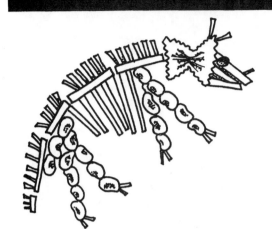

CHAPTER 5

Digging Up Dinosaurs

By Aliki

Aliki. *Digging Up Dinosaurs*. New York: HarperCollins, 1981, 1988. [32 pages]

Describes how fossil hunters find, retrieve, and prepare dinosaur bones for display in museums.

Introduction

Aliki is the author and illustrator of over fifty books for children. Her parents were immigrants to America from Greece. Aliki grew up speaking Greek and did not learn English until she entered elementary school at the age of six.

In exploring *Digging Up Dinosaurs*, the book club can focus on dinosaurs, fossils, and archeologists; or focus its attention upon the author. If the latter option is chosen, *Digging Up Dinosaurs* would then be one example of the outstanding nonfiction work by this author and artist. Refer to "Other Titles to Share" in this chapter for a listing of other books by Aliki on dinosaurs and fossils.

Begin the session by serving Greek food (see "Snacks") and providing writing paper and pencils or crayons. Ask the children to write Aliki a letter telling her how much they enjoyed *Digging Up Dinosaurs*. Decorate letters with an illustration of a dinosaur. Play Greek folk music to set the mood for introducing the author.

Share the author's biographical information and book talk the autobiographical picture book *Marianthe's Story: Painted Words/Spoken Memories*. *Marianthe's Story* is a unique title because it is two separate stories bound into one book (see "Other Titles to Share" in this chapter).

Introduce and dramatize fables that are attributed to the Greek slave Aesop, such as *The North Wind and the Sun* and *The Lion and the Mouse*. End the session with the book discussion questions for *Digging Up Dinosaurs*.

Another option is to conduct the book discussion, host a visiting archeologist (fossil hunter), and end with the Dinosaur Noodle Skeleton craft (see Figure 5.2, page 64).

Introducing the Author/Illustrator

Aliki

Photo by Val Lambros. Courtesy of HarperCollins Publishers.

It took three years for Aliki to write and illustrate *Digging Up Dinosaurs*. "Those illustrations took a long time because of all the bones," says Aliki.

The book started with excursions to the Museum of Natural History in New York City. Her children were very small when she first visited the museum. Aliki asked the other children, who were also there, why they liked the dinosaur skeletons. They answered that the dinosaurs were big, bony, and dead.

From her research, Aliki first wrote *My Visit to the Dinosaurs* (HarperCollins, 1969, 1985) followed by three other books about dinosaurs, including *Digging Up Dinosaurs*.

"I never do a book unless I'm interested in the subject," says Aliki. "I love archeology. I am curious about things. I didn't know anything about dinosaurs when I started. . . . Children can dig into books and find out—just like me."

One interesting fact the author uncovered in her research about dinosaurs is that there were two different kinds. The differences between the dinosaurs are based upon their hips. Aliki wrote about this fact in her book *Dinosaurs Are Different* (Crowell, 1985).

Aliki researches and asks lots of questions so she can convey thought-provoking and fun information through text and illustration. Readers delight in the unique facts that she uncovers.

"I find answers so children can find out," says Aliki. "I'm not a scientist or an expert, so I read and ask. When someone says the dinosaurs were big—how big? Big as a truck? I want to know."

Aliki considers herself an illustrator first and then a writer. She wanted to be an artist since she was a young girl attending kindergarten. To date, she has not written a book without artwork. The illustrator puts friends and family members in her illustrations, and her children Jason and Alexa Demetria are in most of her books. The young girl, with the sketchpad, narrating *Digging Up Dinosaurs* is Aliki herself.

"I never thought I'd be a writer, but I started expressing my feelings in third grade whenever I was hurt, angry, or happy. My writing started from there," says Aliki.

She grew up in Philadelphia but was born in Wildwood Crest, New Jersey, during her parent's vacation. James and Stella Liacouras, her parents, emigrated from Greece to the United States as children. Aliki grew up in a tight-knit family, speaking Greek. She did not learn English until she entered elementary school. *Marianthe's Story: Painted Words/Spoken Memories* is autobiographical and *Painted Words* is based upon the illustrator's experience at school.

"The mother [in *Painted Words*] looks like my mother, and some of her words could be my mother's and my grandmother's," says Aliki.

The school featured in the illustrations is Bell Avenue School, where Aliki attended as a young girl. The teacher is a combination of two "great teachers" that Aliki met during author visits to the United States: Debe Petrey in Ohio and Tim Hamilton in Tennessee. The dedication page in *Painted Words* reads, "For those dedicated, unsung teachers who change and enrich lives."

"In the book, I decided to make the teacher a man so there would be a father figure in juxtaposition to the mother character," says Aliki.

Several years ago, Aliki and her family moved to England. The author/illustrator visits the United States often and speaks at schools, libraries, and conferences. She is married to Franz Brandenberg, who is also the author of many books for children. Most of them are illustrated by his talented wife.

The author welcomes correspondence from children and teachers. Her contact information is: Aliki Brandenberg, 17 Regent's Park Terrace, London, NW1 7ED, England.

Discussion Questions

Make sixteen photocopies of the *Triceratops* on yellow paper (see Figure 5.1, page 60). Reproduce the questions (page 61) on white copy paper; cut and glue them to the back of the dinosaurs. Laminate, if possible, and cut along the outlines of the *Triceratops*.

Pass the discussion questions around in a small basket. The *Triceratops* should be face up with the questions hidden from view. Have one child select a dinosaur from the basket, read the question aloud, and give his or her opinion or answer. If desired, the discussion can be opened to the group for others to give their viewpoints or thoughts. Then the child passes the basket to the next individual who repeats the process. Allow only one *Triceratops* to be drawn at a time. This prevents others from reading and concentrating on their questions and not listening to what is being discussed

Remember, some of the discussion questions have more than one answer, or there is no "right" answer. Children may voice a completely different response than expected.

Figure 5.1. Triceratops for Discussion Questions

Discussion Questions

Describe a museum that you have visited.	Do you think *Tyrannosaurus rex* was a meat eater or a plant eater?
How small was the smallest dinosaur?	What did dinosaurs eat?
What are fossil hunters?	Where do fossil hunters find dinosaur bones?
Why does the photographer take pictures of the bones in the ground?	How are the bones packed for shipping to the museum?
What does the scientist do with dinosaur bones?	How do you make a dinosaur skeleton?
Why are museums important?	Would you like to build a dinosaur skeleton? Why or why not?
Which is your favorite dinosaur? Why?	A plant-eating dinosaur has what kind of teeth—flat or sharp?
Which is your favorite illustration?	What do you like best about Aliki's book, *Digging Up Dinosaurs*?

Activities

Meet Aliki and Share Her Greek Heritage

Begin this activity by introducing the biographical information about Aliki. End with the information that Aliki's parents were from Greece and that she grew up speaking Greek first. She later learned English when she entered elementary school. Briefly booktalk *Marianthe's Story: Spoken Memories / Painted Words* (see "Other Titles to Share"), and make copies of the book available for checkout at the end of the session.

Using a world map or globe, show the students where Greece is located. Introduce fables that are attributed to the Greek slave Aesop, who lived from 620–560 B.C. Refer to the following book: Webber, Desiree et al. *Travel the Globe: Multicultural Story Times*. Illustrated by Sandy Shropshire. Englewood, Colorado: Libraries Unlimited, 1998, 244 pages. (For preschool through third grade.)

An entire chapter in *Travel the Globe* is devoted to Greece. Recommended titles, games, crafts, and storytelling devices related to Greece are provided. For example, patterns for making stick puppets to tell "The North Wind and the Sun" and "The Lion and the Mouse" are included, along with the written stories to be read.

An alternative to the stick puppets is to have the children dramatize the fables as you narrate them. Many of the fables are short and will allow most of the children opportunities to participate.

✓ **IDEAL STORIES FOR THIS PROJECT ARE:**

- "The North Wind and the Sun": Needs a cast of three. A suggested prop is a cloak. This can be created with a tablecloth, a towel, or a coat.

- "The Lion and the Mouse": Needs a cast of two. Suggested prop is a net. Hot-gluing strips of macramé rope together can create a net, or just use a tablecloth as a substitute.

- "The Man, the Boy and the Donkey": Needs a cast of three. No props.

- "The Tortoise and the Hare": Needs a cast of six. Suggested props are a four-foot piece of ribbon or rope for the finish line and a trophy. One cast member is the tortoise, the other the hare. Two people hold the finish line, one person is the judge who awards the trophy, and the remaining individual plays the part of the cheering crowd. If you have remaining children who need parts, add them to the cheering crowd.

✓ **FOR COLLECTIONS OF AESOP'S FABLES REFER TO THE FOLLOWING TITLES:**

- *Aesop's Fables*. Illustrated by Michael Hague. New York: Holt, Rinehart and Winston, 1985. [28 pages]. Brief renditions of Aesop's fables with the moral stated at the end of each one.

- Clark, Margaret. *The Best of Aesop's Fables*. Illustrated by Charlotte Voake. Boston: Little, Brown, 1990. [61 pages]. A nice collection of well-known and lesser-known fables are presented in this title.

Write to the Author Activity

As a take-home project, or as an extending activity for the classroom, children can write to Aliki.

Provide pencils and writing paper for the group. If a child would rather send a drawing, provide crayons or markers and drawing paper. Children can tell Aliki Brandenburg that they read her book *Digging Up Dinosaurs* for their book club.

Tell the group that the author lives in London, England, and locate it on a map or globe. Explain that the letters will be mailed together directly to Aliki's home.

In choosing to write to Aliki, plan ahead to do this book early in the book club series. It will allow Aliki enough time to respond before the series of book club meetings are finished. Children will enjoy receiving a response to their letters.

Include a cover letter and write about the book club group and what the children are doing. Provide return postage as a courtesy. Doing this may also assist in a speedy reply. The author travels extensively, so timing will play a part in planning this exercise.

Contact information is 17 Regent's Park Terrace, London, NW1 7ED, England.

Visiting Fossil Hunter

Invite an archeologist from your state's Archeological Survey, local college, or natural history museum to speak to your book club. Check the government or business section of your phone book to locate the telephone number(s). To ensure that your speaker will be interesting to children, ask for an individual who has experience with school or library visits.

Some government agencies have individuals who visit schools and libraries at no charge as part of their outreach efforts. A good speaker will have hands-on items to share, such as fossils excavated from sites within the state.

When making arrangements with the speaker, confirm the date of the presentation, what time the speaker should arrive, how long the speaker is expected to speak, and what information will be covered. Ask what equipment is needed, such as a slide projector and screen or television and VCR. Provide a table for hands-on items. Confirm that the presentation is free or confirm the price for the presentation.

Make certain that the speaker has the address of where the program will take place plus a telephone number to call in case a problem arises. Ask the speaker for a mailing address and tell the speaker you will send a letter of confirmation. See a sample letter of confirmation in the *Rattlesnake Dance* chapter, page 187.

A week before the scheduled presentation, call the speaker and again confirm the date, time, and location. Have a backup activity in case an emergency or illness prevents your speaker from visiting that day.

After the presentation, be sure to write a thank-you note, or send thank-you notes written by the children. Speakers enjoy this meaningful gesture of appreciation.

Note for school media specialists and teachers: If you call a speaker that is some distance away, arrange for him or her to spend a couple of hours at the school. The speaker can speak to several classrooms or make a couple of presentations in the media center. Arrange for lunch before your speaker returns to his or her office.

Craft

Dinosaur Noodle Skeleton Craft

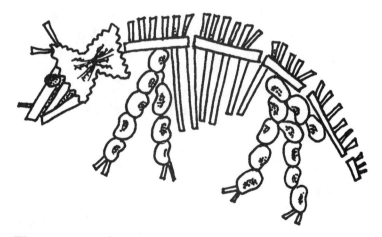

Figure 5.2. Dinosaur Noodle Skeleton Sketch

✓ **SUPPLIES**

8½-by-11-inch heavyweight poster board

Different types of pasta: spaghetti, fettuccini, macaroni, bow tie, and so forth

Different types of dried beans: lima, pinto, split pea, and so forth

White glue

Wax paper

Toothpicks

During the craft session, play the cassette tape version of Aliki's *Digging Up Dinosaurs*. (HarperChildren's Audio, 1991, 18 min., ISBN: 1-55994-302-5.)

Provide each child with a piece of poster board, a variety of pasta and dried beans, a square of wax paper with a dab of white glue the size of a quarter, and a toothpick. Also make available pictures of dinosaurs. To prevent damage to books or other visual aids, photocopy pictures and allow the children to keep them near the area where they are working.

Children will use their imaginations to create a skeleton for their chosen dinosaur. Using the toothpick, they will dab or smear glue onto the pasta (or beans) and place them on the poster board. Write the name of the dinosaur at the bottom of the poster board along with the child's name. Allow the artwork to lie flat until dry. Display in the library for all to view.

Snacks

Fresh fruit and yogurt

Feta cheese

Butter cookies or baklavá

In celebration of Aliki's Greek heritage, serve fruit and yogurt, cheese, and pastry treats. Grapes are a major agriculture product of Greece, and stuffed grapes leaves is a popular dish there. Be sure to include grapes in the fruit and yogurt dish. Feta cheese is made from goat milk and can be served with pita bread or crackers. Ancient Greeks were one of the first to develop baked pastries. Bake or purchase butter cookies or, as a special treat, serve the traditional honey and nut pastry—baklavá.

Fruit and Yogurt Recipe

INGREDIENTS

4 cups chopped fruit (e.g., apple, pear, peach, etc.)
1 cup strawberry- or peach-flavored yogurt

DIRECTIONS

Mix together and chill. Makes six servings.

Other Titles to Share

Aliki. *Dinosaurs Are Different*. New York: HarperCollins, 1985. [32 pages]

Differences between dinosaurs are determined by examining their bones. For example, some dinosaurs have hips like a lizard and others have hips like a bird.

———. *Dinosaur Bones*. New York: Thomas Y. Crowell, 1988. [32 pages]

In 1822, Mary Ann Mantell discovered fossilized teeth. Since then, scientist have been excavating and studying dinosaurs bones to learn all they can about these "terrible lizards."

———. *Fossils Tell of Long Ago*. New York: Thomas Y. Crowell, 1972, 1990. [32 pages]

Describes how different types of fossils are made and what they tell scientists about the plants, insects, and animals that lived long ago.

———. *Marianthe's Story: Painted Words; Marianthe's Story: Spoken Memories*. New York: Greenwillow Books, 1998. [Two books bound as one; each book is 32 pages]

In *Spoken Memories*, young Mari tells her class about life in the country she left in order to come to the United States. *Painted Words* is autobiographical about the author's experience in elementary school.

———. *My Visit to the Dinosaurs*. New York: HarperCollins, 1969, 1985. [32 pages]

A young child tells the reader about fossils, the work of paleontologists, and the dinosaur exhibits that one might see at a museum.

Brighton, Catherine. *The Fossil Girl: Mary Anning's Dinosaur Discovery*. Brookfield, CT: Millbrook Press, 1999. [32 pages]

A true story about the young girl who discovered a fossilized ichthyosaur in Dorset, England, in 1810.

Cole, Joanna. *The Magic School Bus in the Time of the Dinosaurs*. Illustrated by Bruce Degen. New York: Scholastic, 1994. [48 pages]

Ms. Frizzle and her class take a drive back in time beginning with the Triassic period and the early dinosaurs.

Digging Up Dinosaurs. Great Plains National Instructional Television Library and WNED-TV. Produced by Lancit Media Productions. 30 min. Stamford, CT: Children's Video Library, 1986. Videocassette.

The Reading Rainbow presentation of Aliki's *Digging Up Dinosaurs*.

Dodson, Peter. *An Alphabet of Dinosaurs*. Illustrated by Wayne D. Barlowe and Michael Meaker. New York: Scholastic, 1995. [66 pages]

Contains uncommon dinosaurs such as the *Xenotarsosaurus*. Color paintings and black-and-white illustrations of skeletons and skulls accompany the brief text.

Grambling, Lois G. *Can I Have a Stegosaurus, Mom? Can I? Please!?* Illustrated by H. B. Lewis. Mahwah, NJ: Bridgewater Books, 1995. [32 pages]

A young boy tells his mother all the wonderful ways a *Stegosaurus* could help him.

Hartmann, Wendy, and Niki Daly. *The Dinosaurs Are Back and It's All Your Fault Edward!* Illustrated by Niki Daly. New York: Margaret K. McElderry Books, 1997. [32 pages]

A humorous tale about an older brother who tries to scare his younger brother by convincing him the rock under his bed is a dinosaur egg.

Hoff, Syd. *Danny and the Dinosaur.* New York: HarperCollins, 1958, 1986, 1993. [64 pages]

Danny visits a museum and finds a live dinosaur to play with. An easy-to-read book.

Contacting the Publisher

Contact the marketing department of HarperCollins at 1350 Avenue of the Americas, New York, NY 10019, 212-261-6500, http://www.harpercollins.com. Ask what promotional items they have for *Digging Up Dinosaurs* such as posters, bookmarks, and the author's biography. Request enough supplies for each child in your book club and your files.

CHAPTER 6

The Great Kapok Tree: A Tale of the Amazon Rain Forest

By Lynne Cherry

Cherry, Lynne. *The Great Kapok Tree: A Tale of the Amazon Rain Forest*. San Diego: Harcourt Brace Jovanovich, 1990. [32 pages]

A great number of valuable products are produced from kapok trees. When a man comes into the jungle to cut down one of them, the animals that live in that tree must convince him not to destroy their home.

Introduction

Rain forests make up less than one-twentieth of the Earth's landmass, but scientists say that the plants and animals inhabiting rain forests account for more than half of the species on our planet. With the great number of plants and trees in these areas, rain forests are an important source of oxygen for the world, and significant medicines continue to be developed from the plants that grow there.

Even young children are aware of the need to conserve the Earth's environment and to protect the world's wildlife. Reading such books as Cherry's *The Great Kapok Tree* and discussing the issues encompassing the destruction of the rain forests can help young people better understand the need to preserve them.

Begin this session by serving snacks with a tropical flair. Children can have fun with the Animals of the Kapok Tree Crossword Puzzle (Figure 6.2, page

74) or the Rain Forest Word Scramble (Figure 6.3, page 76) as an option to snacks, or do both. Consider playing taped sounds of jungle animals or pipe music from Peru [Runa Pacha, *Tarpuy: Musica de Los Andes*, Condor Productions, n.d. Compact disc. Contact José Muenala, 1325 Dupard Street, Mandeville, LA 70448, 504-626-4816, fax 504-674-6838]. Peru borders Brazil and is the location where headstreams form the great Amazon River. Water from melting snows and glaciers, high in the Andes Mountains, meet near Iquitos, Peru, to create the world's second-longest river.

Proceed with one of the suggested activities such as Futbolito or Portuguese Hopscotch on pages 75 and 77. Discussion questions will lead to a quieter, contemplative period. Craft time can be next. If the schedule allows, encourage the children to act out *The Great Kapok Tree* using the stick puppet patterns that the children make or you provide (see Figures 6.6A–6.6J, pages 80–84).

Introducing the Author/Illustrator

Photo by Aldo Brando. Courtesy of Harcourt, Inc.

Lynne Cherry

As a child, Lynne Cherry spent as much time as she could in the woods near her home. She remembers many happy hours playing and experiencing nature while learning of the plant and animal world around her. When she had to be indoors, young Cherry was drawn to reference books about animals, studying the drawings and photographs with intense interest. As an adult, those loves dominate the lifework of Cherry, as her writing and illustration projects continue to represent those resolute beliefs in the importance of protecting the world's environment and wildlife.

After graduating in 1973 from the Tyler School of Art in Philadelphia, Pennsylvania, Cherry began illustrating for others. In a few short years, at the young age of twenty-three, she progressed to illustrating and writing her own books. Her medium of choice has always been watercolor. From the very beginning, Cherry's work has represented her profound regard for nature.

When Cherry was creating the story line for *The Great Kapok Tree*, she traveled to Brazil's rain forest to study and paint the animals and plants. Because she spoke Spanish (much like the Portuguese language spoken in Brazil), she was able to work with the native people who were also interested in making others aware of the need to protect the beauty there.

While in Brazil, Cherry learned of Chico Mendes, to whom she dedicated *The Great Kapok Tree*. "He had tremendous personal strength and stood up for what he felt was right ... protecting his homeland (the rain forest) from destruction."

The Great Kapok Tree has earned numerous awards and is a Reading Rainbow featured title. In addition, Cherry has created another work on the rain forest theme titled, *The Shaman's Apprentice: A Tale of the Amazon Rain Forest* (see "Other Titles to Share" in this chapter).

Speaker, teacher, and environmentalist, Lynne Cherry works closely with the Smithsonian Institution and the National Museum of Natural History in Washington, D.C., and is currently developing The Center for Children's Environmental Literature, of which she will be the director. She spends much of her time in programs that embrace her desire to make the world a better place.

"Outdoors has been my life," expresses Cherry, "and I am *still* learning about the natural world. I want children, as well, to know about the beauty and wonder of the plants and animals of the world. It's important for them to think beyond themselves and to always remember that the Earth—its people, its animals, its environment—is a sacred place."

Cherry spends time on her farm in Maryland when she is not in Washington, D.C. or traveling. Contact her through the publisher: Harcourt Inc., 525 B Street, Suite 1900, San Diego, CA 92101-4495.

Discussion Questions

Make sixteen photocopies of the Morpho butterfly (Figure 6.1, page 72) on blue paper. If desired, highlight the edges of the wings with a dark blue or black chalk, pastel or colored pencil. Reproduce the questions (page 73) on white copy paper. Cut and glue them to the backs of the butterflies. Laminate, if possible, and cut along the outlines of the butterflies.

Pass the discussion questions around in a small basket or upturned safari hat. The butterflies should be face up with the questions hidden from view. Have one child select a butterfly from the basket, read the question aloud, and give his or her opinion or answer. If desired, the discussion can be opened to the group for others to give their viewpoints or thoughts. Then the child passes the basket to the next individual who repeats the process. Allow only one butterfly to be drawn at a time. This prevents others from reading and concentrating on their questions and not listening to what is being discussed.

Remember, some of the discussion questions have more than one answer, or there is no "right" answer. Children may voice a completely different response than expected.

Activities

Animals of the Kapok Tree Crossword Puzzle

Photocopy the activity sheet (Figure 6.2, page 74) for each child in the book club. Answers to the activity are on page 75.

Figure 6.1. Morpho Butterfly for Discussion Questions

Discussion Questions

Would you like to visit a rain forest? Why or why not?	What are the three main levels of a rain forest?
Which animal had the best reason to save the kapok tree?	Which is your favorite illustration? Why?
Why did the animals become quiet when the man woke up?	Name some things the kapok tree could be used for after being cut down.
Read aloud Lynne Cherry's dedication of this book. Talk about who you think this man is or what he did.	There are no highways or television in the rain forest. Is it quiet or noisy there?
Would you want to live in a rain forest? What would you like the most? The least?	Which animal in the story would you want to be?
How did reading *The Great Kapok Tree* change the way you think about the environment and rain forests?	How is a kapok tree different from trees in your neighborhood?
What did the Yanomamo boy mean when he said, "When you awake, look upon us with new eyes"?	What do you think happened after the man left the forest?

Note: The World Book Encyclopedia *has short, informative articles about the kapok tree and Chico Mendes, which could help the moderator guide discussion.*

Animals of the Kapok Tree
Crossword Puzzle

Directions: Look at the pictures in *The Great Kapok Tree* for hints to the puzzle's answers.

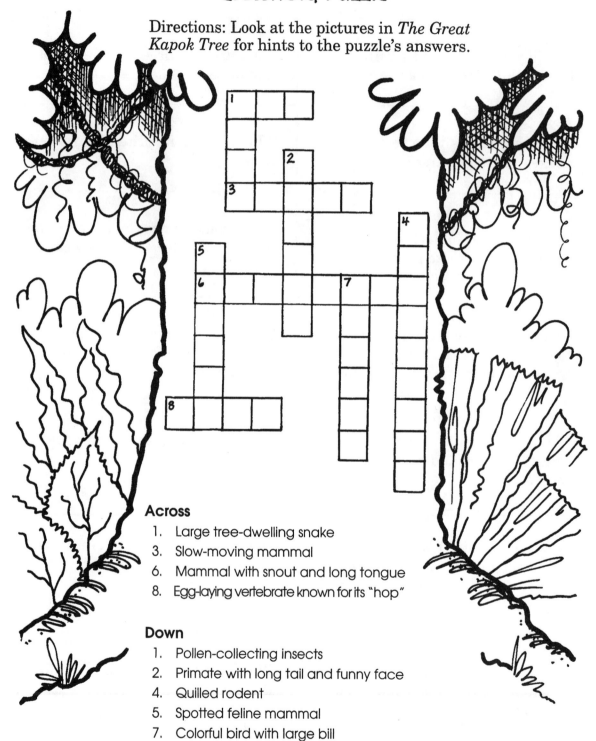

Across

1. Large tree-dwelling snake
3. Slow-moving mammal
6. Mammal with snout and long tongue
8. Egg-laying vertebrate known for its "hop"

Down

1. Pollen-collecting insects
2. Primate with long tail and funny face
4. Quilled rodent
5. Spotted feline mammal
7. Colorful bird with large bill

Figure 6.2. Animals of the Kapok Tree Crossword Puzzle

Crossword Puzzle Answer Key

Across	**Down**
1. Boa	1. Bees
3. Sloth	2. Monkey
6. Anteater	4. Porcupine
8. Frog	5. Jaguar
	7. Toucan

Rain Forest Word Scramble

Photocopy the activity sheet (Figure 6.3, page 76) for each child in the book club. Answers to the activity are below.

Rain Forest Word Scramble Answer Key

1. TAPIR	7. FLOWERS
2. IGUANA	8. VINES
3. PARROT	9. YANOMAMO BOY
4. OCELOT	10. PARAKEET
5. WOOLLY MONKEY	11. TREES
6. BLUE MORPHO	

Futbolito (Little Soccer) Game

✓ SUPPLIES

A grapefruit, orange, or rolled up sock

Small objects to mark the goal area

A defined space for the playing field

Futbol (soccer) is a popular sport in Brazil. Children too poor to own a soccer ball might use a substitute, such as those listed above, to play the game. Define a small playing area. Twelve feet by twelve feet is sufficient for four to six players. Mark two goal areas, no more than one to two feet in width, at opposite ends. Remind players that pushing is not allowed. Teamwork is paramount. If you have a large group of children, consider making several teams made up of three or four children.

Children use only their feet to kick the "soccer ball" around the field and past the goal line. No use of hands is allowed. One point is scored for every goal. Play for a set time period, such as ten minutes.

Children can select names for their teams from *The Great Kapok Tree*, such as Jumpin' Jaguars or Tough Toucans. Winning teams are those with the most points by the end of the time period.

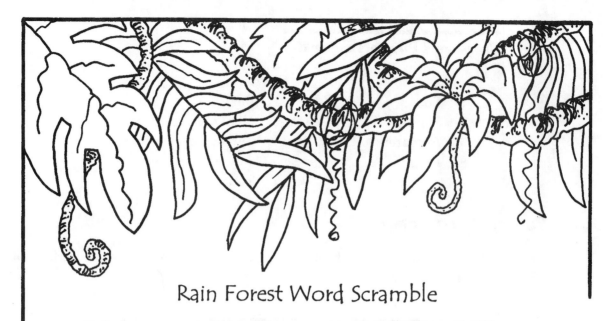

Rain Forest Word Scramble

Below are words from Lynne Cherry's book *The Great Kapok Tree*. See how many you can unscramble. Write the correct word on the lines next to the scrambled word. For example, G R O F would be written F   R   O   G .

1. PARIT __ __ __ __ __

2. AANUGI __ __ __ __ __ __

3. RAPROT __ __ __ __ __ __

4. TOELCO __ __ __ __ __ __

5. LOWLOY KEYMON __ __ __ __ __ __ __ __ __ __ __ __

6. LUBE PROMOH __ __ __ __ __ __ __ __ __ __

7. OWLFRES __ __ __ __ __ __ __

8. NIVES __ __ __ __ __

9. MANYMOOA YOB __ __ __ __ __ __ __ __ __ __ __

10. RATKEEPA __ __ __ __ __ __ __ __

11. REETS __ __ __ __ __

Figure 6.3 Rain Forest Word Scramble

Portuguese Hopscotch Game

Figure 6.4. Portuguese Hopscotch Game Pattern

✓ **HOPSCOTCH VOCABULARY AND PRONUNCIATION GUIDE**

Monday	**segunda-feira**	se-GOON-dah FAY-rah
Tuesday	**terca-feira**	TAIR-sah FAY-rah
Wednesday	**quarta-feira**	KWAR-tah FAY-rah
Thursday	**quinta-feira**	KEEN-tah FAY-rah
Friday	**sexta-feira**	SAYSH-tah FAY-rah
Saturday	**sábado**	SAHB-adō
Sunday	**domingo**	DŌ-min-gō
The sky	**o céu**	ōh SAY-oo
The world	**o mundo**	ōh MOON-dō

✓ **SUPPLIES**

Pucks for throwing (flat stones or pieces of orange peel; approximately 2 by 2 inches)

Chalk (if a concrete surface) or masking tape (if a carpet or tile surface)

This is a fun way to have a little exposure to the Portuguese language, the national language of Brazil. Using strips of orange peel for pucks emphasizes the tropical fruits found in rain forests. Orange peel is also a very effective puck because it does not roll when tossed. Children may write their intials on their pucks with a permanent marker.

Depending on floor's surface, use chalk or masking tape to create the hopscotch pattern as shown in Figure 6.4 (page 77). The finished hopscotch is between seven and nine feet. For several players, more than one hopscotch pattern will be needed. Four players per pattern is the maximum number—everyone gets to play without too much waiting between turns and too many pucks in the pattern will make it difficult to jump.

The first player begins the game by throwing his or her puck into the first block, marked *segunda-feira*. The player must throw the puck so that it lands in the correct block without touching any lines. If successful, the player begins jumping using one foot or two feet (as determined by the pattern). The player cannot jump into the block with the puck or touch any of the lines with his or her feet. (If the player is not successful, the turn ends, and the next player tries.)

The player travels up the hopscotch, turns around at the end (outside of the last block), and travels back down the hopscotch. When the player arrives at the block containing his or her puck, the player must bend down to pick it up and continue jumping through the beginning square. (Sometimes the person must bend down on one leg. If the player loses his or her balance and steps into another square or touches a line, the player's turn is over.)

If the first player is successful in navigating the hopscotch, he or she throws the puck to the next square, *terca-feira*, and jumps through the pattern again. This process is repeated until the first player gets to the *o mundo* block or commits an error, such as the puck not falling into the right block, the puck touching a line, a player touching a line with his or her foot, or a player losing his or her balance. Once the player has committed an error, his or her turn is over and the player places the puck in the last successful block—not the block the player tried and missed.

The next player repeats the process listed above. However, in addition to jumping over his or her own puck, the player must jump over any pucks belonging to the other players. Sometimes a player has to jump over a section of blocks and reach back to retrieve his or her own puck.

The first player to reach the last block is the winner. The game can be extended by having the players travel from *segunda-feira* to *o mundo* and then back again from *o mundo* to *segunda-feira*.

Craft

Kapok Tree Animal Stick Puppets

✓ **SUPPLIES**

Crayons, pastels and/or markers

Glue sticks or cool glue gun (for adult use only)

Large-size craft sticks

Scissors

Copy paper, tag board, or construction paper

Figure 6.5. Stick Puppet Sketch

Using Figures 6.6A–J (pages 80–84), make enough photocopies so that everyone in the group can have an animal to color, cut out, and attach to a craft stick (Figure 6.5). If desired, enlarge the patterns. For an even more creative experience, children may want to develop their own animals.

Photocopying patterns onto colored paper will lessen the amount of coloring that the children feel they must accomplish. Paper colors do *not* have to match the color of the animal in nature. Children will add color to meet their expectations.

When the stick puppets are completed, consider reading *The Great Kapok Tree* aloud so that the children listen to what their animals ask the sleeping man.

If time allows, and the group is agreeable, put on a play. Additional props can be added: a kapok tree constructed of brown and green butcher paper, a cardboard axe, and additional animals. Be sure to read Lynne Cherry's introduction to set the mood.

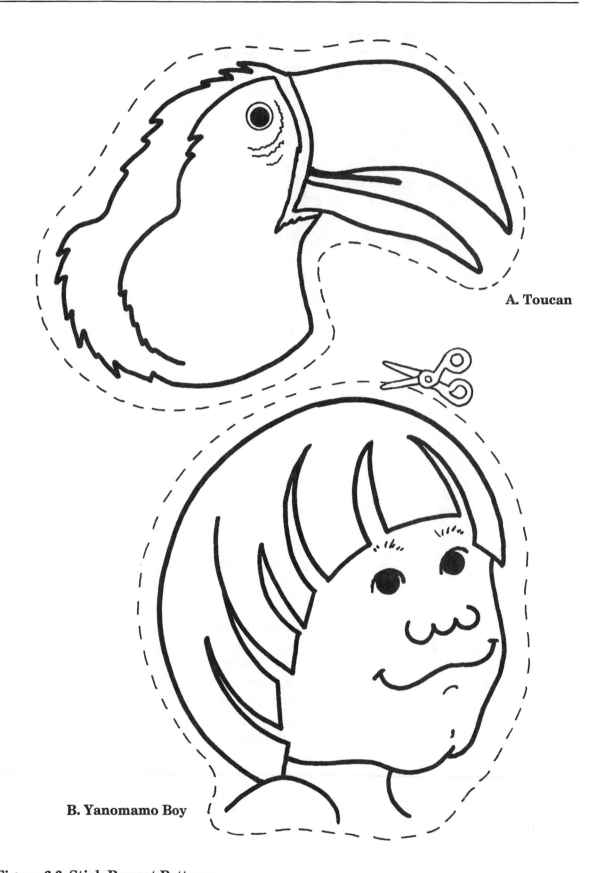

A. Toucan

B. Yanomamo Boy

Figure 6.6. Stick Puppet Patterns

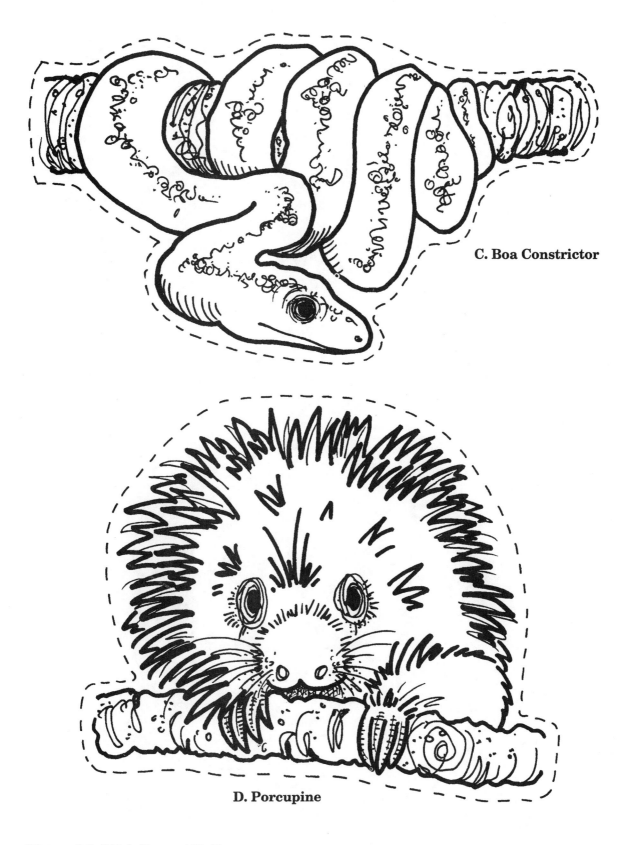

C. Boa Constrictor

D. Porcupine

Figure 6.6. Stick Puppet Patterns

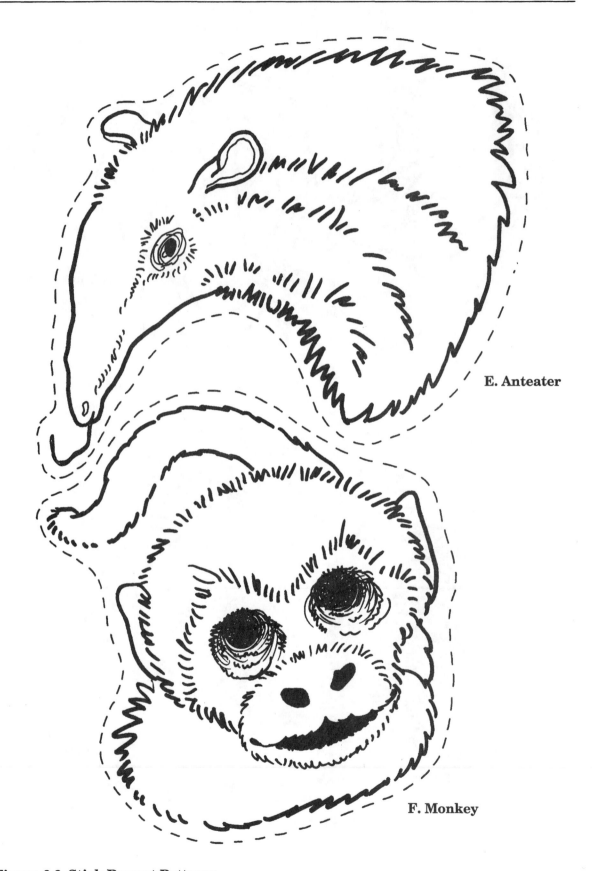

E. Anteater

F. Monkey

Figure 6.6. Stick Puppet Patterns

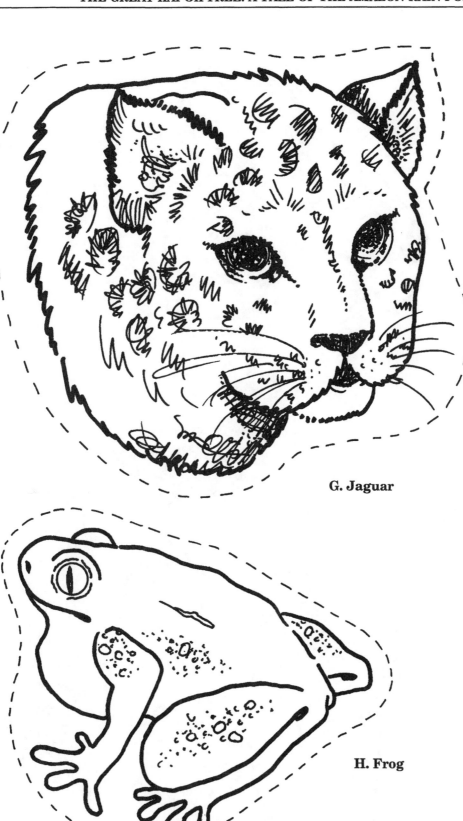

G. Jaguar

H. Frog

Figure 6.6. Stick Puppet Patterns

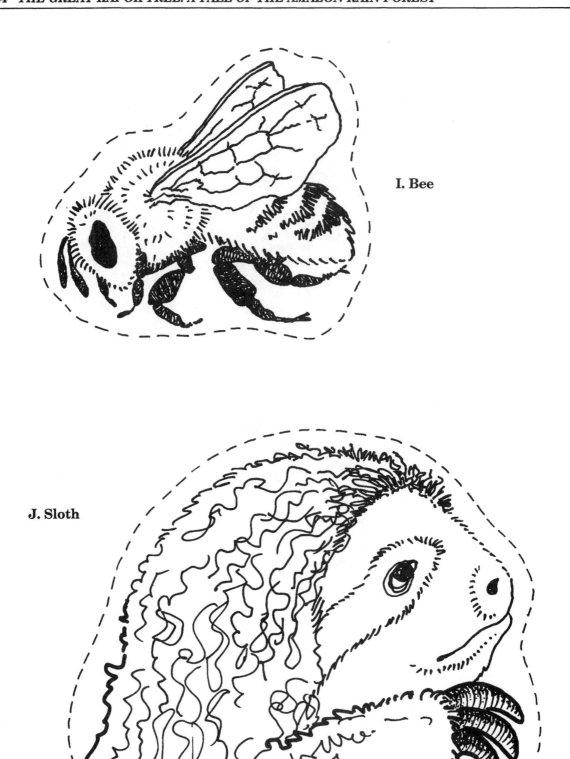

I. Bee

J. Sloth

Figure 6.6. Stick Puppet Patterns

Snacks

Fruit juice

Nuts (Make sure none of the children have an allergy to nuts.)

Coconut candy balls (see recipe)

Chocolate bananas (see recipe)

Rain Forest Fast Food (see serving suggestions)

Coconut Candy Balls Recipe

INGREDIENTS

1 cup granulated sugar
¼ cup of water
1 cup shredded coconut

DIRECTIONS

Mix the sugar and water in a saucepan and cook over medium heat. Stir constantly until it reaches the "soft ball" stage or when a candy thermometer registers 230–240 degrees. Remove from heat and beat mixture with the spoon for thirty to forty seconds. Add the coconut and beat for another thirty seconds. Pick up a soupspoon full, form a ball, use another spoon to help shape, and then scoop it off onto a plate to cool. Makes 12.

Chocolate Bananas Recipe

INGREDIENTS

6 bananas   12 small, wooden craft sticks
Chocolate syrup

DIRECTIONS

Peel the bananas and cut them in half crosswise. Push a small, wooden craft stick into the cut end of each piece and put them into the freezer for an hour. Cover the cold bananas with chocolate syrup using either a dipping or pouring process. When the coating sets, lay them on a piece of aluminum foil or a tray, and place in the freezer until ready to serve. Makes 12.

Rain Forest Fast Food

Serve small chunks of fruit or vegetables on a hand-size piece of banana leaf (available in some local markets or health food stores). Substitute with a lettuce leaf, if something tropical is not available, or cut a leaf pattern from green paper for the "plate." If fruit is served, sprinkle a bit of flaked coconut over the top. Fruits can include chunks of orange, apple, mango, pineapple, and coconut.

Sweet potatoes are a staple with most families in Amazon rain forests, so consider baking one and adding small chunks of it along with raw white potato and carrot for a vegetable version of Rain Forest Fast Food.

Other Titles to Share

Baker, Lucy. *Life in the Rain Forests*. Chicago: World Book, 1990, 1997. [32 pages]

Photographs and illustrations feature the animals and indigenous people and plants, along with terms, issue questions, and a sample quiz. A folk tale from the African Congo is also included.

Burch, Joann J. *Chico Mendes, Defender of the Rain Forest*. Brookfield, CT: Millbrook Press, 1994. [48 pages]

A brief biography of a native Brazilian who devotes his life to the preservation of the Amazon rain forest.

Cherry, Lynne, and M. J. Plotkin. *The Shaman's Apprentice: A Tale of the Amazon Rain Forest*. Illustrated by Lynne Cherry. San Diego: Harcourt Brace, 1998. [36 pages]

Inhabitants of the Tirio Indian village of Kwamala learn that their shaman's knowledge of medicinal plants is useful to others outside the Amazon rain forest. The shaman passes on his wisdom to a younger member of the village.

Clarke, Penny. *Rain Forest*. Illustrated by Carolyn Scrace. New York: Franklin Watts, 1996. [39 pages]

A comprehensive, well-illustrated overview that touches on issues concerning threats to the continued existence of rain forests. Index included.

Gibbons, Gail. *Nature's Green Umbrella: Tropical Rain Forests*. New York: Morrow Junior Books, 1994. [29 pages]

Succinctly describes the plants and animals of the rain forest ecosystem. Illustrated with colorful drawings.

Get to Know Lynne Cherry. Produced by Rosemary Killen. 20 min. San Diego: Harcourt Brace, 1993. Videocassette.

An inspirational presentation on how Lynne Cherry's work and dreams have helped others realize their responsibility to save the world's natural resources. Filmed in the many locations from which the author draws ideas for her books.

The Great Kapok Tree: A Modern Fantasy Picture Book Video. Based on the book written and illustrated by Lynne Cherry. Produced by Rosemary Killen. 9:27 min. New York: SRA/McGraw-Hill, 1996. Videocassette.

This is an animated video production in which rain forest animals that make a kapok tree their home convince a man not to chop it down.

Lasky, Kathryn. *The Most Beautiful Roof in the World: Exploring the Rain Forest.* Photographs by Christopher G. Knight. New York: Harcourt Brace, 1997. [45 pages]

A joint project by an award-winning husband and wife team documenting Dr. Meg Lowman's work in a rain forest canopy.

Lessem, Don. *Inside the Amazing Amazon.* Illustrated by Michael Rothman. New York: Crown, 1995. [34 pages]

Fold-out cross sections of the Amazon River region represent a brilliant look at the floor, understory, canopy, and emergent layer of the rain forest.

Osborne, Mary Pope. *Afternoon on the Amazon.* Illustrated by Sal Murdocca. New York: Random House, 1995. [67 pages]

Jack and Annie are magically whisked to the Amazon River where they encounter crocodiles, vampire bats, killer ants, and many adventures. Number six of the Magic Tree House series.

Pirotta, Saviour. *People of the Rain Forest.* Austin, TX: Raintree Steck-Vaughn, 1999. [32 pages]

Amazing photographs give insights into the indigenous people of the world's rain forests: how they hunt and farm, festivals they celebrate, foods that are enjoyed, plus the different types of homes. A face painting project, a glossary, a bibliography, and useful addresses are included.

Riley, Peter, and Sherry Gerstein. *Nightwatch: Nightlife in the Tropical Rain Forest.* Illustrated by Barry Croucher and Brin Edwards. Pleasantville, NY: Reader's Digest Children's Books, 1999. [17 pages]

In a unique, see-through window format, photographs and paintings portray the mysterious creatures of the nighttime rain forest jungle of South America's Amazon Basin.

Totally Tropical Rain Forest. Narrated by Dudley Moore. Really Wild Animals series. 40 min. Washington, DC: National Geographic Society, 1994. Videocassette.

"Spin," National Geographic's animated globe-on-the-go, leads a trip to the rain forests of Central and South America. Shows the variety of wild animals that can be found, from the forest floor to the treetop canopy.

Weeks, Sarah. *Piece of Jungle.* Illustrated by Suzanne Duranceau. New York: HarperCollins, 1999. [30 pages]

Tropical rain forest animals are the focus of this book. The verses to a song by the author are the text.

Yolen, Jane. *Welcome to the Green House.* Illustrated by Laura Regan. New York: G. P. Putnam's Sons, 1993. [32 pages]

Tropical rain forest ecology is presented in this beautiful picture book full of rhythmic language.

Contacting the Publisher

Contact the marketing department at Harcourt Inc., 525 B Street, Suite 1900, San Diego, CA 92101-4495, 619-261-6616, http://www.harcourtbooks.com. Ask what promotional items they have for *The Great Kapok Tree: A Tale of the Amazon Rain Forest* such as posters, bookmarks, and the author's biography. Request enough supplies for each child in your book club and your files.

CHAPTER 7

Home Run: The Story of Babe Ruth

By Robert Burleigh

Illustrated by Mike Wimmer

Burleigh, Robert. *Home Run: The Story of Babe Ruth*. Illustrated by Mike Wimmer. San Diego: Harcourt Brace & Company, 1998. [32 pages]

This picture book contains two tales in one. The first story tells of Babe's love for the game as he hits a home run. The second story, told on baseball cards, gives Babe's biography.

Introduction

Almost everyone enjoys attending a good game of baseball. The smells of hot dogs, roasted peanuts, and cotton candy fill the air of a cool summer night. One by one, batters approach home plate to meet the challenge of knocking a leather sphere out of the ballpark. Spectators cheer, sing, clap, and stomp as their team heroes go to bat. *Home Run* by Burleigh and Wimmer, introduces readers to one of baseball's greatest players—Babe Ruth.

George Herman Ruth not only played baseball with great enthusiasm, but he lived life the same way. He ate huge meals, spent money freely, and loved to attend parties. Ruth was the undisputed king of baseball. He could pitch, catch, run, and hit.

In 1927, Ruth hit a record sixty home runs in one season. His outstanding performance withstood competition for thirty-four years until Roger Maris hit sixty-one home runs in 1961. The Babe also batted a lifetime record of 714 home runs. This record remained unchallenged until 1974 when Henry Aaron batted 715 career home runs.

The Yankees released Ruth in 1934. The baseball legend wanted to turn manager but his offer was not accepted.

Begin this session by serving snacks and distribute either the Make That Catch! Hidden Pictures (Figure 7.2, page 95) or the Home Run Word Scramble (see pages 96–97). Once everyone has gathered, play Take Me Out to the Ball Game Musical Chairs. Introduce the author and illustrator and moderate the book discussion session. End with the Our Favorite Team Pennant craft (Figure 7.6, pages 98–99) session.

Introducing the Author and Illustrator

Robert Burleigh

Photo by Sharon Hoogstraten. Courtesy of Harcourt, Inc.

Robert Burleigh lives in a loft apartment in Chicago, Illinois, near Lake Michigan. For the past thirty-five years he has written adult fiction, poetry, and books for children. Burleigh began his career developing educational filmstrips, videos, and cassettes. He became a full-time author in 1994.

The author began writing in college but following graduation he lived a vagabond life. Burleigh held many jobs, including schoolteacher and working in a hotel kitchen. His first children's picture book was *A Man Named Thoreau* (Atheneum, 1985) followed by *Flight: The Journey of Charles Lindbergh* (Philomel, 1991).

Mike Wimmer illustrated *Flight*. During a promotional book tour, Burleigh and Wimmer met. The two became acquainted and their friendship led to the joint project of *Home Run: The Story of Babe Ruth*. The book was published on the fiftieth anniversary of Babe Ruth's death and in the same year that Mark McGwire and Sammy Sosa broke Roger Maris's home run record.

Born on January 4, 1936, Burleigh is married and has three children. Write to Burleigh c/o Harcourt Inc., 525 B Street, Suite 1900, San Diego, CA 92101.

Mike Wimmer

Photo by Mike Wimmer. Courtesy of Harcourt, Inc.

In preparing the paintings for *Home Run*, Wimmer gathered Babe Ruth memorabilia. When deciding in what year of Babe Ruth's career to set the illustrations, Wimmer chose 1927 and had a seamstress sew the Yankee uniform from that year.

"Illustrations show more than what the text says," says Wimmer. "The wrinkles around Babe's eyes say something. People thought Babe was on his way out in 1927. The Yankees were thinking of getting rid of him." That year, Babe Ruth hit a record sixty home runs.

Wimmer often uses family and friends in his work. His son Eli was the model for the young Babe Ruth and, in the painting showing the crowd, a neighbor of Wimmer's has his finger over the camera lens.

This talented illustrator was born in Muskogee, Oklahoma, on March 22, 1961, and lives today in Norman, Oklahoma with his wife Carmelita and two children. "I always wanted to be a professional football player," said Wimmer. Instead he became a professional artist and an illustrator of children's books.

Young Wimmer began drawing and painting at six years of age. His stepfather worked for Container Corporation of America in Muskogee, Oklahoma. He brought home the ends of paper rolls used to create cardboard boxes. "These rolls of brown paper, to make boxes, were nine to ten feet in diameter," says Wimmer. "Close to the end of a run, when the paper was almost gone, they would install a new roll. My stepdad would bring home these rolls, with the leftover paper, and I would draw and paint on them."

Wimmer illustrated mainly famous athletes and comic book figures, but the art of N. C. Wyeth, Harvard Pyle, and Norman Rockwell inspired him. Following high school, Wimmer studied art at the University of Oklahoma and spent two years on a commercial art apprenticeship at the well-known Sketchpad Studio in Arlington, Texas. His grandfather told him that he would excel at doing what he loved—the wise gentleman was right.

Contact Mike Wimmer at 2005 North Grassland Drive, Norman, OK 73072 or through his Web site http://www.mikewimmer.com.

Discussion Questions

Make sixteen photocopies of the baseball graphic (Figure 7.1, page 93) on white paper. Highlight the stitching on the graphic with a bright red marker. Reproduce the questions (page 94) on white bond paper. Cut and glue them to the back of the baseball graphics. Laminate, if possible, and cut along the outlines of the baseballs.

Pass the discussion questions around in a baseball cap. The baseballs should be face up with the questions hidden from view. Have one child select a baseball from the baseball cap, read the question aloud, and give his or her opinion or answer. If desired, the discussion can be opened to the group for others to give their viewpoints or thoughts. Then the child passes the baseball cap to the next individual who repeats the process. Allow only one baseball to be drawn at a time. This prevents others from reading and concentrating on their questions and not listening to what is being discussed.

Remember, some of the discussion questions have more than one answer, or there is no "right" answer. Children may voice a completely different response than expected.

Activities

Take Me Out to the Ballgame Musical Chairs

✓ **SUPPLIES**

Chairs

Cassette or compact disc player

Music: "Take Me out to the Ball Game" (One source for finding or purchasing the music is: Raffi. *One Light, One Sun*. Toronto, ON, Canada: Troubador Records, 1985. Available from Kimbo Educational, 800-631-2187.)

Before starting, explain the game to the group. This activity is fast, fun, and creates much laughter.

To begin the game, place chairs in two rows with the backs of the chairs together. You will always have one less chair than the number of players. For example, if you have sixteen children you will start with fifteen chairs.

As you play the music, the children walk in a circle around the chairs. When the moderator stops the music, each child tries to take a seat. The one who does not get a chair is out of the game. Another chair is removed and the process begins again.

Eventually, the game ends with two players circling a single chair. When the music stops, the child who is able to sit down wins. Prizes are not necessary. Just give the winner a round of applause.

Make That Catch! Hidden Pictures Puzzle

Photocopy the puzzle activity sheet (Figure 7.2, page 95) for each child in the book club.

Figure 7.1. Baseball for Discussion Questions

Discussion Questions

How did Ruth get the nickname "Babe"?	Why is Babe Ruth famous?
What other nicknames did Babe Ruth have?	Which is your favorite picture? Tell us why.
Describe Babe Ruth.	Who is your hero? Why?
Tell us about your favorite baseball team.	How did Babe Ruth make so many home runs?
What promise did Babe Ruth make to a sick boy?	Tell us something that you are proud of achieving.
Where did Babe Ruth grow up?	What do you like best about this book?
Some people collect baseball cards. What do you collect?	What is your favorite sport?
What is something you want to be good at in the future?	How many eggs could Babe Ruth eat for breakfast?

Make That Catch!

Help the outfielder find the following hidden items: bat, jersey numbers 3 and 7, cup of lemonade, batting helmet, home plate, popcorn, first base, hot dog, cotton candy, peanut, pennant, and baseball.

Figure 7.2. Make That Catch! Hidden Pictures Puzzle

Figure 7.3. Make That Catch! Hidden Pictures Answer Key

Home Run Word Scramble

Photocopy the activity sheet (Figure 7.4, page 97) for each child in the book club. Answers to the activity are below.

Home Run Word Scramble Answer Key

1. BABE RUTH
2. BASEBALL
3. BAT
4. BALL
5. BASE
6. SCORE
7. HOME RUN
8. SWING
9. CAP
10. MITT
11. CROWDS
12. PEANUTS
13. CHEERS
14. UMPIRE

Home Run Word Scramble

Below are baseball-related words. See how many you can unscramble. Write the correct word on the lines next to the scrambled word. For example, P I R E U M would be written U̲ M̲ P̲ I̲ R̲ E̲.

1. E A B B U T R H ___ ___ ___ ___   ___ ___ ___ ___

2. L L B A S E A B ___ ___ ___ ___ ___ ___ ___ ___

3. T B A ___ ___ ___

4. L A B L ___ ___ ___ ___

5. S A B E ___ ___ ___ ___

6. E S O R C ___ ___ ___ ___ ___

7. R N U H M O E ___ ___ ___ ___   ___ ___ ___

8. S W N I G ___ ___ ___ ___ ___

9. P A C ___ ___ ___

10. T T I M ___ ___ ___ ___

11. S D W O R C ___ ___ ___ ___ ___ ___

12. T U N S P E A ___ ___ ___ ___ ___ ___ ___

13. C H E E S R ___ ___ ___ ___ ___ ___

14. P I R E U M ___ ___ ___ ___ ___ ___

Figure 7.4. Home Run Word Scramble

Craft

Our Favorite Team Pennant Craft

Figure 7.5. Pennant Sketch

✓ **SUPPLIES**

Pennant pattern (Figure 7.6)

Construction paper (enough for one pennant per child)

Scissors

White glue

Cool glue gun (adult use only) or adhesive tape

Crayons or non-permanent magic markers

Dowel rods (¼ inch in diameter, 18 inches in length)

To save time, pre-cut a pennant for each child. Select a variety of colors from which to choose. Light-colored paper, such as yellow, pink, white, blue, and orange, work the best when using crayons and markers to decorate. Attach the pennants to the dowel rods using a cool glue gun.

Introduce the craft by showing the children an official team pennant or creating a sample pennant using the pattern and construction paper. Ask the children to create their own pennants using magic markers, crayons, and pieces of construction paper from which to cut shapes and letters to glue. Each child can create a pennant representing his or her favorite team (any sport).

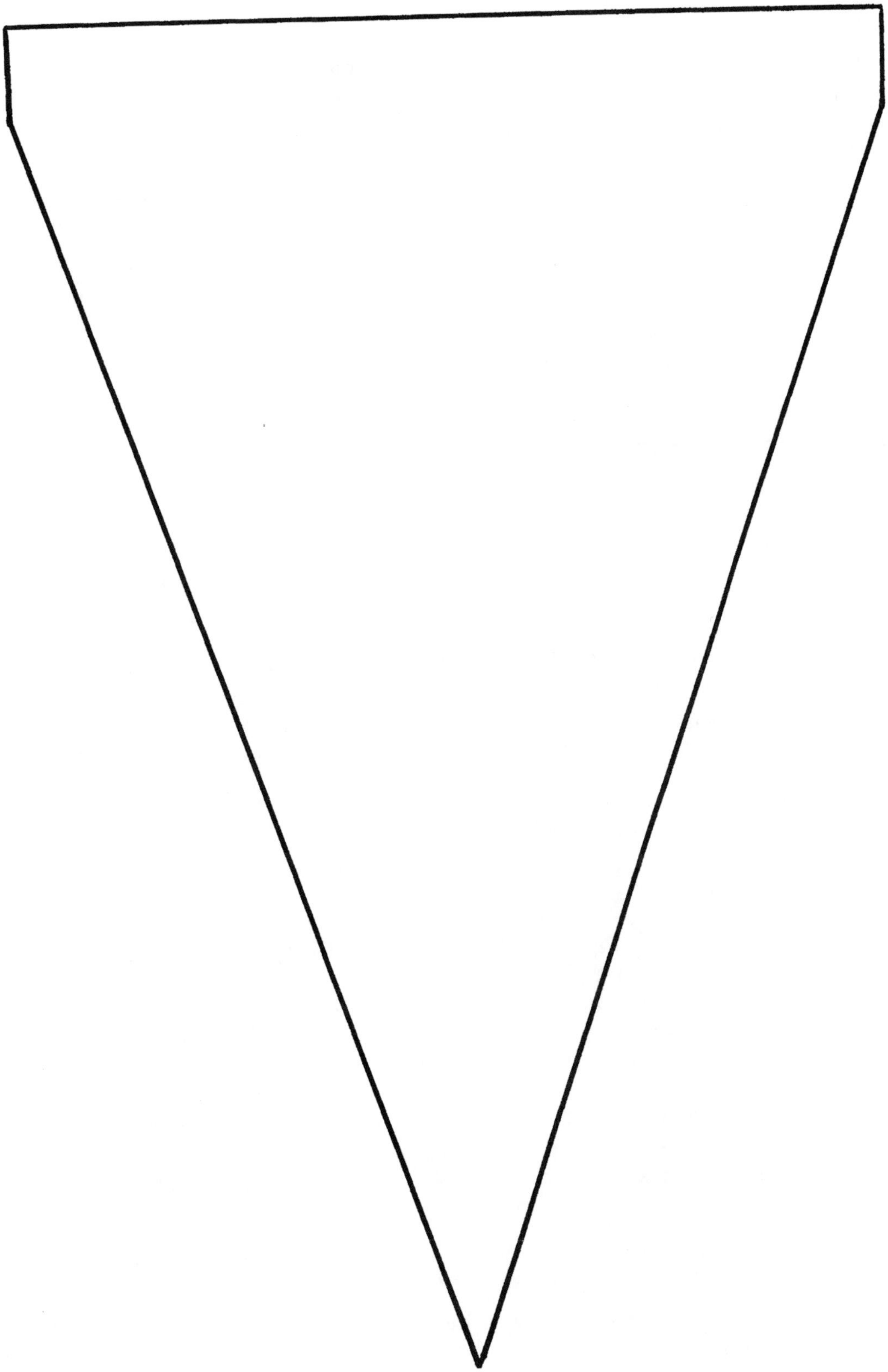

Figure 7.6. Pennant Pattern

Snacks

People love to eat during a baseball game. Choose one or more of the following favorite items or purchase a candy bar for each attendee. A particular candy bar was named after the "Sultan of Swat"—Babe Ruth.

Individual boxes of carmeled popcorn

Roasted peanuts in the shell (Before bringing these in, be sure no one in the group is allergic to peanuts or peanut dust.)

Popcorn

Lemonade or fruit juice

Other Titles to Share

Adler, David A. *The Babe & I*. Illustrated by Terry Widener. San Diego: Harcourt Brace, 1999. [32 pages]

With the help of Babe Ruth and the Yankees, a young boy helps his family earn money during the depression.

——. *Cam Jansen and the Mystery of the Babe Ruth Baseball*. Illustrated by Susanna Natti. New York: Puffin Books, 1991, 1982. [57 pages]

Cam Jansen and her friend Eric Shelton track down the thief who stole a baseball signed by Babe Ruth from a hobby show at the local community center.

Bottner, Barbara. *Nana Hannah's Piano*. Illustrated by Diana Cain Bluthenthal. New York: G. P. Putnam's Sons, 1996. [32 pages]

Nana Hannah helps her grandson develop a musical talent along with his love for baseball.

Curtis, Gavin. *The Bat Boy and His Violin*. Illustrated by E. B. Lewis. New York: Simon & Schuster, 1998. [32 pages]

Reginald's father is the coach of the Dukes—the worst team in the Negro leagues of 1948. His father wants him to put aside the violin and help as bat boy, but soon realizes his son's music talent is helping the team to victory.

Kovalski, Maryann. *Take Me out to the Ballgame*. New York: Scholastic, 1992. [32 pages]

The well-known song by Jack Norworth is brought to life by Kovalski's humorous illustrations showing a grandmother taking her two granddaughters to a baseball game.

Kraus, Robert. *Mort the Sport*. Illustrated by John Himmelman. New York: Orchard Books, 2000. [32 pages]

Mort likes sports and playing the violin, but doing both leads to an unexpected ending.

Krensky, Stephen. *Arthur Makes the Team: A Marc Brown Arthur Chapter Book*. Illustrated by Marc Brown. Boston: Little, Brown, 1998. [61 pages]

Arthur has missed a season of baseball practice and does not feel he is as good as the other players. Francine's teasing makes the situation worse.

Parish, Peggy. *Play Ball, Amelia Bedelia*. Illustrated by Wallace Tripp. New York: HarperCollins, 1996, 1972. [64 pages]

The Grizzlies need one more player and Amelia Bedelia volunteers to help, even though she does not know how to play.

Rappaport, Doreen, and Lyndall Callan. *Dirt on Their Skirts: The Story of the Young Women Who Won the World Championship*. Illustrated by E. B. Lewis. New York: Dial Books for Young Readers, 2000. [33 pages]

Using a fictional family, Rappaport retells the women's championship ball game of September 16, 1946, between the Illinois Rockford Peaches and the Wisconsin Racine Belles.

Thayer, Ernest Lawrence. *Casey at the Bat*. Illustrated by Barry Moser. Boston: David R. Godine Publisher, 1988. [32 pages]

There are many editions of this famous American poem. Moser's illustrated version celebrates 100 years of the poem's existence, and Donald Hall writes an afterword with historical notes about the author and the times.

Contacting the Publisher

Contact the marketing department of Harcourt Inc., 525 B Street, Suite 1900, San Diego, CA, 92020, 619-699-6716, http://www.harcourtbooks.com. Ask what promotional items they have for *Home Run* such as baseball cards, the author's and illustrator's biographies, bookmarks, and posters. Request enough supplies for each child in your book club and your files.

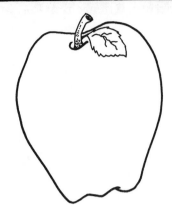

CHAPTER 8

Johnny Appleseed

By Steven Kellogg

Kellogg, Steven. *Johnny Appleseed*. New York: Morrow Junior Books, 1988. [42 pages]

The legendary life of American folk hero John Chapman is presented in this delightfully illustrated picture book.

Introduction

American tall tales are about exciting heroes and heroines. One of those tall-tale heroes was nicknamed Johnny Appleseed. He roamed the eastern and midwestern United States all of his adult life—more than forty years—planting apple seeds and sharing his generous nature and love of life.

John Chapman was born in 1874, and at a very young age had a mission in mind. He was determined to see apple trees growing all over the new America to supply westward-moving pioneers with needed food on their difficult journeys. Legends tell us that this gentle, peace-loving individual went barefoot and carried no gun or knife, even though he walked alone in the wilderness. Instead of a hat, he wore his cooking pan on his head! Some of the trees that Johnny Appleseed planted in Pennsylvania, Ohio, Kentucky, Illinois, and Indiana are still producing apples today.

October is National Apple Month and would make an ideal month to schedule this session. Begin the program with the Johnny in the Woods Maze (Figure 8.3, page 110) and serve apple-related snacks.

Proceed with the lively Apple Heads Relay Game (see page 111), which can be great fun even with limited space. Set the mood for the game by playing recorded music of Gioacchino Rossini's *William Tell* Overture. (Gioacchino Rossini, *Favorite Overtures*, Stuttgart Radio Symphony Orchestra: Gianluigi Gelmetti. EMI Electrola GmbH, 1992. Compact disc.) Share the story of William Tell, who shot an apple off his son's head with an arrow. If you are not familiar with the legend from Switzerland, look at the *World Book Encyclopedia* for a quick summary or read the picture book version *William Tell* by Leonard Everett Fisher (see "Other Titles to Share" in this chapter), and retell it to the group.

Introduce author and illustrator Steven Kellogg using information from this chapter or the videocassette *Trumpet Video Visits Steven Kellogg* (see "Other Titles to Share"). The video is seventeen minutes long—all or part of the video may be shown. (Contact customer service at Weston Woods at 1-800-543-7843.) Proceed with the discussion questions and end with either the Johnny's Apple Beasties Craft (Figure 8.4, page 112) or the Johnny Appleseed Mural (Figure 8.5, page 113). As an alternative, consider the apple bobbing and apple toss activities. When the children leave, give each an apple lapel badge to wear home. See Figure 8.1 (page 106) for a template to create the badge.

In conducting this session, a supply of apples may be needed. Consider contacting grocery stories, local fruit stands, regional orchards, or generous parents for donations; or ask the children to bring one or two apples with them.

Introducing the Author/Illustrator

Steven Kellogg

Photo by Alan S. Orling. Used by permission of HarperCollins.

Even as a preschooler, with crayon in hand, Steven Kellogg wanted to make drawing his life's work. This award-winning illustrator has created art for more than 100 books. Of these, he has authored more than thirty, and the book projects continue.

What inspired Kellogg to become one of the most respected and recognized illustrators of children's picture books? In reflection, he relates that there was much encouragement from his family. Two younger sisters were often entertained with an activity called "Telling Stories on Paper," in which Steven told inventive tales while producing masses of drawings.

At an early age, he remembers that his aunt enrolled him in the Junior Literary Book Club. This contributed to a lifelong love for literature and reading. Young Kellogg especially loved animal stories such as *Black Beauty*, *King of the Wind*, and the Beatrix Potter titles. Books about famous people were also favorites.

However, not all his time was spent indoors reading and sketching. With childhood friends, he played "magical kingdom" in the woods near his home. "I loved the outdoors as a kid and still do."

Kellogg was born on October 26, 1941, and grew up in Connecticut. His formal education includes a degree from the Rhode Island School of Design. The winning of a special fellowship in his senior year allowed him to go to Florence, Italy, to further develop his artistic skills. After graduate school and some university teaching, Kellogg began sending his picture-book ideas to publishers. He had not forgotten his childhood dream to create "story pictures."

His first book appeared in 1967 and many years later Kellogg says that he is still passionate about creating illustrations and telling stories. His *Johnny Appleseed* is part of a series on America's tall-tale heroes and heroines published by HarperCollins. Other titles include *Pecos Bill*, *Paul Bunyan*, *Sally Ann Thunder Ann Whirlwind Crockett*, and *Mike Fink*.

"John Chapman was a gentle folk hero. He was different from most tall-tale characters, who were often confrontational," says Kellogg. "Not Johnny Appleseed. He was a lover of the wilderness and aware of the problems of the pioneers.

"One of my favorite illustrations in this book is the double-page spread of Johnny and the approaching pioneers. He's feeling happy because he knows he is aiding these people with the gift of the enduring apple tree. I believe his message to us might have been to be kind and love nature."

Other best-loved Kellogg books include *Island of the Skog* (Dial, 1973), *The Mysterious Tadpole* (Puffin Pied Piper, 1977), and his retold classics of *Chicken Little* (Morrow Junior Books, 1985) and *The Three Little Pigs* (Morrow Junior Books, 1997). His work has received many awards, including several titles featured on the *Reading Rainbow* television program.

Steven Kellogg and Helen Kellogg have raised six children, and now count eight grandchildren in their family. Most of his books have been dedicated to his children, grandchildren, and friends. The couple lives in Sandy Hook, Connecticut, in their rural, hillside farmhouse. Summers are spent at a studio in Essex, New York.

Numerous family pets have appeared in Kellogg's books. There have been many large, spotted Great Dane dogs, as seen in the Pinkerton series, and the current cocker spaniel as seen in *Best Friends*. The likenesses of various household cats have also appeared in numerous illustrations.

Kellogg suggests watching the Weston Woods video titled *Trumpet Video Visits Steven Kellogg* (see "Other Titles to Share") to know him better. Children may write to Steven Kellogg c/o HarperCollins Publishers, 1350 Avenue of the Americas, New York, NY 10019.

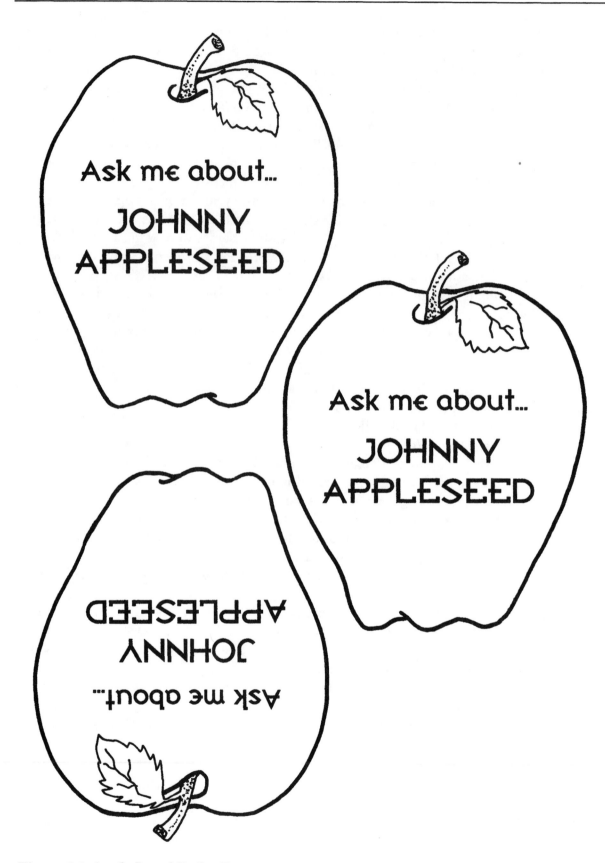

Figure 8.1. Apple Lapel Badge Pattern

Discussion Questions

Make sixteen photocopies of the apple (Figure 8.2, page 108) on red paper. If desired, use green, yellow, and orange colors to represent varieties of apples. Reproduce the questions (page 109) on white copy paper. Cut and glue them to the back of the apples. Laminate, if possible, and cut along the outlines of the apples.

Pass the discussion questions around in a small basket or an old cooking pot with a handle. The apples should be face up with the questions hidden from view. Have one child select an apple from the basket, read the question aloud, and give his or her opinion or answer. If desired, the discussion can be opened to the group for others to give their viewpoints or thoughts. Then the child passes the basket to the next individual who repeats the process. Allow only one apple to be drawn at a time. This prevents others from reading and concentrating on their questions and not listening to what is being discussed.

Remember, some of the discussion questions have more than one answer, or there is no "right" answer. Children may voice a completely different response than expected.

Activities

Johnny in the Woods Maze

Photocopy the activity sheet (Figure 8.3, page 110) for each child in the book club.

Figure 8.2. Apple for Discussion Questions

Discussion Questions

There are many kinds of apples. How many varieties can you name?	Do you think Johnny Appleseed was a pioneer or an explorer? Look in a dictionary to help you decide.
What is the difference between a story and a tall tale?	Which is your favorite illustration?
At a young age, John Chapman knew what he wanted to do. What do you want to be when you grow up?	Some of the trees Johnny Appleseed planted are still growing. How old is an apple tree planted in 1820?
Name some of the states in which Johnny Appleseed planted trees.	What is your favorite way to eat apples?
What does it take to grow an apple tree?	Why were apple trees important to frontier settlers?
In what season are apples ripe and ready to pick?	What do you like best about Johnny Appleseed?
Describe the good things about Johnny Appleseed's life.	Describe the bad things about Johnny Appleseed's life.
Johnny Appleseed lived to be seventy years old. Do you know anyone that age?	Would you have liked being Johnny Appleseed? Why or why not?

Johnny in the Woods

Johnny Appleseed wants to take a nap under the shady tree. Can you help him find his way through the giant apple maze?

Figure 8.3. Johnny in the Woods Maze

Apple Heads Relay Game

Divide the group in half, and direct them to line up at the starting point. (Place a strip of tape on the floor for participants to wait behind.) Teams might want to choose a team name, such as the "Appleseed Athletes" or "Johnny's Joggers."

Play a small portion of Gioacchino Rossini's *William Tell* overture. Ask the group if they are familiar with the music. Gioacchino Rossini's *William Tell* overture makes great accompanying race music. [Gioacchino Rossini, *Favorite Overtures*, Stuttgart Radio Symphony Orchestra: Gianluigi Gelmetti. EMI Electrola GmbH, 1992. Compact disc.] The appropriate section of the overture to play during the race occurs during the last three minutes. If the equipment is available, record this part twice on a cassette tape for ease of access during the races. Play the cassette tape recording to begin the race. If the *William Tell* overture is not available, substitute with other lively music

Explain the rules of the game: Each person balances an apple on the top of his or her head, walks to the turnaround point, returns to the starting point, and hands off the apple to a teammate.

To add a bit of whimsy, place a chair or an upside-down bucket (an apple-picking bucket, of course) at the turnaround point.

At the turnaround, each player must sit down and loudly exclaim, "Apples are a tasty treat!" before returning to the starting line. Children will want to play this game more than once!

Apple Bobbing or Apple Toss Games

Bobbing for apples is always fun. A large, water-filled tub and apples to float in the water are all that is needed. Close supervision is necessary with children.

An apple toss can be another simple activity; however, cutting holes in heavy cardboard or plywood will take some time. Apple-shaped beanbags can be substituted for the real thing. Ask someone who sews to make apple beanbags from heavy-duty felt or fabric. If using real apples, lay a blanket behind the board to cushion the fall of the fruit. Assign point values to the openings.

To play, have the children stand behind a line made on the floor with masking tape. The line can be from four to eight feet from the backboard, depending on the general skills of the group. The adult moderator decides if two, three, or four tosses will determine an individual's turn. Children can keep their scores on a chalkboard or large tablet.

Crafts

Johnny's Apple Beasties Craft

Figure 8.4. Johnny's Apple Beasties Sketch

✓ **SUPPLIES (for each beastie)**

1 apple

5 round toothpicks

5 gumdrops (red or variegated colors)

4 whole cloves

Fruit leather or construction paper (maximum 2-by-2-inch piece)

Shoestring licorice or pipe cleaner (any color, 3 inches in length)

Scissors

Small, thin-bladed knife (for adult use only)

Each child will carefully push a toothpick through one of gumdrops and then poke it into the *bottom* of the apple to form a snout. Push a toothpick into each of the four gumdrops. Press into the appropriate places to make feet. (If this is difficult for young children, an adult can press the gumdrops into place.)

Push in two cloves for eyes and two cloves in the gumdrop snout for the nostrils. Twist off the apple's stem, poke a hole with a toothpick and insert the 3-inch-long piece of shoestring licorice or pipe cleaner to form a tail. The toothpick can be used to thrust the licorice securely into the hole. (Remove the toothpick when finished.) The tail can be straight or curled.

Cut two small ears from construction paper or fruit leather. Ears can be curled or triangle-shaped. Using a thin-bladed knife, the adult cuts two slits into the apple where the ears will go. Allow the child to direct the adult where to cut the slits. Push ear pieces into the openings.

When finished, the participants can tell the group what kind of beasties they have created, and what kind of encounter Johnny Appleseed might have had with them. See Figure 8.4 for an example of the finished craft.

Johnny Appleseed Mural

Figure 8.5. Johnny Appleseed Mural Sketch

✓ **SUPPLIES**

8 feet of white butcher paper

Brown and green construction paper

Non-permanent markers

Red tempera paint or non-permanent ink pads

2-inch-wide paintbrush (if using the tempera paint)

Plastic plates or old cookie sheets (if using the tempera paint)

Apples cut in half (one half per child)

Scissors

Glue

For this group project, have ready a length of wide butcher paper with the slogan, "Thank You Johnny Appleseed" running lengthwise through the middle. Letters can be cut from brown (or any color) construction paper, or use paint or markers to make the words. (For easy cleanup, cover the work area with newspaper or plastic tablecloths.)

Also, prior to the session, cut leaves from green construction paper. Make several for each child in the group. Cut apples in half from top to bottom.

For the craft, children will make apple prints, glue leaves, and write words or short sentences on the mural. To make apple prints, give each child a half apple. Press apples into red, non-permanent ink pads and then press onto the white butcher paper. If ink pads are not available, an adult can brush a thin layer of red tempera paint onto old cookie sheets or plastic plates. Children can then press apple halves into paint.

After making the apple prints, children can glue several green leaves around the border and write words about apples or a simple phrase to John Chapman. Attach the mural to a wall for all to enjoy.

Snacks

Apple tea (recipe follows) or apple cider
Johnny's Hat Applesauce

Other snack ideas: apple slices dipped in chocolate, apple jelly or apple butter on bread or crackers, bottled apple cider, dried apple rings, dried apple chunks with raisins, or have a volunteer bake apples, apple pies, or apple tarts.

Apple Tea Recipe

For this drink to have a pleasant taste, select apples that have a good flavor. In past times, this tea was given to someone with a fever. It was also used to quench a serious thirst.

INGREDIENTS

1 tart apple (Granny Smith, Cortland, or McIntosh)
5 cups water (depending on how strong one wants the tea)
Sugar to taste

DIRECTIONS

Wash the apple. Cut into small pieces. Combine with the water in a saucepan and boil until apple is soft. Strain the liquid and add sugar, stirring to dissolve. Serve hot or cold. Makes five servings. Increase recipe to make enough for your group.

Johnny's Hat Applesauce Recipe

Serve from an old pan with a handle. The older the pan looks, the more it will resemble Johnny Appleseed's hat. Provide small bowls or paper cups, and plastic spoons.

INGREDIENTS

5 large apples (Golden Delicious or Winesap)
1 to 1½ cups water
¼ cup sugar
Dash of cinnamon

DIRECTIONS

Peel, core, and quarter the apples. Put a cup of the water into a blender, add a few pieces of apple, and blend for a few seconds. Continue adding the pieces until mushy. Add the sugar and cinnamon. Blend to desired consistency. Add more water for a thinner mixture. Makes four servings. Increase recipe to make enough for each child in your group.

Other Titles to Share

Cooper, Jason. *Apples*. Photographs by Lynn M. Stone. Vero Beach, FL: Rourke Publications, 1997. [24 pages]

> A simple text with clear, full-color photographs describing how apples are grown and processed in North America. Glossary and index are included.

Fisher, Leonard Everett. *William Tell*. New York: Farrar, Straus & Giroux, 1996. [32 pages]

> William Tell refuses to bow down to a bully and must shoot an arrow placed on his son's head.

Gabbert, Lisa. *An Apple Festival: Orchards in Autumn*. New York: Rosen, 1999. [24 pages]

> Gives information about where apples grow and what occurs at small-town apple festivals.

Gillis, Jennifer Storey. *An Apple a Day! Over 20 Apple Projects for Kids*. Illustrated by Patti Delmonte. Pownal, VT: Storey Communications, 1993. [60 pages]

> A variety of projects, recipes, puzzles, games, and crafts are provided, along with simple text and directions.

Gleiter, Jan, and Kathleen Thompson. *Johnny Appleseed*. Illustrated by Harry Quinn. Milwaukee, WI: Raintree Children's Books, 1987. [32 pages]

> A simple biography, that reads like a pleasant picture book, emphasizing the dream that John Chapman strove to achieve.

Hall, Zoe. *The Apple Pie Tree*. Illustrated by Shari Halpern. New York: Blue Sky Press, 1996. [30 pages]

> An easy apple pie recipe follows the picture book story about an apple tree as it grows to maturity and produces fruit.

Hodges, Margaret. *The True Tale of Johnny Appleseed*. Illustrated by Kimberly Bulcken Root. New York: Holiday House, 1997. [32 pages]

> Presents a well-researched and delightfully written tale of John Chapman, better known as Johnny Appleseed. Unique tidbits not found in other versions are included.

Kalman, Bobbie. *Hooray for Orchards!* Illustrated by Barbara Bedell and Cori Marvin. New York: Crabtree, 1998. [32 pages]

Describes the kind of work involved in an orchard, from grafting trees to harvesting the fruit.

Kellogg, Steven. *Paul Bunyan*. New York: Morrow Junior Books, 1984. [40 pages]

Paul Bunyan grows to be the world's largest lumberjack and crosses the country carving out a new country for settlers.

———. *Pecos Bill*. New York: William Morrow, 1986. [40 pages]

Young Bill is raised by a family of coyotes and grows up to be the country's first cowboy.

———. *Sally Ann Thunder Ann Whirlwind Crockett: A Tall Tale*. New York: Morrow Junior Books, 1995 [41 pages]

Sally Ann displays amazing feats of strength that impresses her nine brothers and later her husband, Davy Crockett.

Lawlor, Laurie. *The Real Johnny Appleseed*. Wood engravings by Mary Thompson. Morton Grove, IL: Albert Whitman, 1995. [63 pages]

Biography of the legendary John Chapman who spent his adult life planting apple trees across the eastern and midwestern United States.

Lindberg, Reeve. *The Legend of Johnny Appleseed*. Paintings by Kathy Jakobsen. Boston: Little, Brown, 1990. [32 pages]

Colorful, detailed art illuminate the lilting, rhymed text about the life and legend of John Chapman. Easy to read aloud.

Marzollo, Jean. *I Am an Apple*. Illustrated by Judith Moffat. New York: Scholastic, 1997. [60 Pages]

The life cycle of an apple tree is succinctly depicted from bud to harvest time.

Osborne, Mary Pope. *American Tall Tales*. Wood engravings by Michael McCurdy. New York: Alfred A. Knopf, 1991. [115 pages]

The story of folk hero Johnny Appleseed is one of several American tall tales in this collection.

Trumpet Video Visits Steven Kellogg. Narrated by Steven Kellogg. Produced by Diane Kolyer. 17 min. Norwalk, CT: Weston Woods, 1993. Videocassette.

An endearing insight into the world of Steven Kellogg: his home in Connecticut, his studio, and at a school visit on Author Celebration Day.

Contacting the Publisher

Contact the marketing department at HarperCollins Publishers, which now owns the William Morrow imprint, 1350 Avenue of the Americas, New York, NY 10019, 212-209-7000, http://www.harpercollins.com/hc. Ask what promotional items they have for *Johnny Appleseed* and Steven Kellogg, such as posters, bookmarks, and the author's biography. Request enough supplies for each child in your book club and your files.

CHAPTER 9

On the Day You Were Born

By Debra Frasier

Frasier, Debra. *On the Day You Were Born*. San Diego: Harcourt Brace Jovanovich, 1991. [30 pages]

> *Lyrical language welcomes a newborn to planet Earth. Illustrated with vibrant paper collages representing the natural worlds of plants and wildlife.*

Introduction

Make use of this book by allowing its simple and endearing content to help teach children that a birth is one of the natural miracles of the world in which they live. Newborns can affect not only their human families, but also the world around them. Experiencing some aspects of *On the Day You Were Born* may inspire young readers to gain surprising insight into the all-encompassing phenomenon of the coming of a new baby and its relationship to the Earth's environment.

As the children arrive to the session, hand each a The Earth Welcomed Me Crown (Figure 9.1, page 120). If time is a factor, have the crowns precut and each child's birthday month, day, and year added to the blank space. If time is not a factor, allow the young readers to decorate and complete their own crowns. Adjust and staple the headband to fit each child's head.

All participants, including the adult moderator, will wear a crown proclaiming their special birth dates throughout the program. Consider allowing the children to sit in groups determined by the season in which they were born.

Begin the session by showing the video *Notes Alive! On the Day You Were Born* while the children have snacks. (See "Other Titles to Share" in this chapter. In addition, review the Notes Alive! Enrichment Curriculum for K–3.) If the video cannot be obtained at your library, request a copy through the library's interlibrary loan services. Play a symphonic selection of music or a long-playing version of the "Happy Birthday to You" song.

Where in the World Was I Born? is a quick, but satisfying, activity with very little preparation, and may prove to be very interesting if young readers have birthplaces all over the world (see page 121). An optional activity is the Happy Birthday to Me! Game. It involves more preparation but assures many smiles because of the numerous rounds of the traditional "Happy Birthday to You" song that will be sung. See Figures 9.4A–F for game pattern pieces.

Share Debra Frasier's biographical information from the chapter. Discussion questions are next. During the discussion period, it may be discovered that children can be very expressive and delightfully egocentric about what they know of their birth. Two craft ideas are suggested depending upon the kind of supplies and preparation time that are available: "On the Day I was Born . . ." Booklet (see page 129) and Leafy Family Tree (see page 127).

Introducing the Author/Illustrator

Debra Frasier

Used by permission from Harcourt Brace.

"When I was growing up, my front porch was the wide, sandy beach of the Atlantic Ocean. I believe that has been the greatest influence on my life as a writer," says Frasier.

Her youthful days in Vero Beach, Florida taught her many things, but perhaps the most long-lasting lesson was learning to love and respect nature.

"My brother and I spent many happy years on the beach, swimming in the ocean, constructing sand and driftwood forts and castles, making things with found items. Every morning we would rush out of the house to see what the waves had washed up on the sand. Those things we collected were like treasure to us, because we knew they were from the ocean's mysterious depths or, perhaps, even from some distant land across the sea. We often slept with our swimming suits under our pajamas so that little time would be wasted in our morning races to the beach."

Young Frasier was an artistic child. Her mother was an artist who introduced her daughter to methods of expression, such as oil painting and collage. The latter remains Frasier's favorite medium.

In college, Debra studied art with a career goal of designing interiors. She has, however, designed numerous exteriors. For many years, Frasier has built large, outdoor puppet pageants. Her one-woman and group art shows in the United States and Europe have often integrated fabrics and wind. Some of her "wind puppets" have been over sixty feet tall and have "danced" on mountaintops.

Frasier has been an artist-in-residence in the United States and France, and continues to lecture at conferences and workshops. Her artist-in-education programs emphasize her interest in nature—a combination of natural history and visual arts. She is devoted to introducing art to children so that it may become an important part of their lives.

Frasier began her writing career when she had to spend many quiet days in the hospital waiting for her daughter to be born.

"I had always wanted to do a picture book," she says. "While in the hospital, the idea for *On the Day You Were Born* seemed to find me. I began to think about the aspects and elements of the world that would welcome my baby. I worked on the words and the collage art for over two years. It was very important to me that everything be just right."

After ten years, *On the Day You Were Born* is still in print and over 900,000 copies have been sold. It has received both the Silver Honor of the Parent's Choice Award and the Andrew Carnegie Medal, among other awards. The story also exists in a variety of formats: audiocassette, video, and Braille, plus a Spanish-language version. In 1992, Frasier collaborated with a theatrical company and took the stage production of *On the Day You Were Born* on a tour around the United States. In 1996, the picture book became the basis for an original symphony written by Steve Heitzeg and performed by The Minnesota Orchestra (see "Other Titles to Share" in this chapter).

The author wishes that all children who experience *On the Day You Were Born* will understand that they have an important place on Earth. She hopes parents who hear or share her book will know how special their children are, as well as all children of the world.

"Everyone's special day is the day of their birth," emphasizes Frasier. "Look at a calendar. Be aware of what season of the year that special day fits into. Know what the animals are doing during your birth time. Ask questions of the people who were waiting for you to be born—your mom and dad, your adoptive parents, grandparents, brothers and sisters, or others."

Frasier's home is now in Minneapolis, Minnesota where she lives with her artist/photographer husband and daughter Calla. The author welcomes correspondence through her Web site at www.frasierbooks.com or through the publisher, Harcourt Inc. at 525 B Street, Suite 1900, San Diego, CA 92101-4495.

Figure 9.1. The Earth Welcomed Me Crown Pattern

Discussion Questions

Make sixteen photocopies of the infant (Figure 9.2, page 122) on a mix of pink and blue paper. Reproduce the questions (page 123) on white copy paper. Cut and glue them to the back of the infants. Laminate, if possible, and cut along the outlines of the babies.

For fun, consider placing a small receiving blanket into a basket so that the infant graphics can be swaddled in the fabric. Be prepared for some antics! Some young readers may pretend that their "baby" is crying or needs a diaper change when they select a question from the basket.

The infant graphics should be face up with the questions hidden from view. Have one child select an infant from the basket, read the question aloud, and give his or her opinion or answer. If desired, the discussion can be opened to the group for others to give their viewpoints or thoughts. Then the child passes the basket to the next individual who repeats the process. Allow only one baby to be drawn at a time. This prevents others from reading and concentrating on their questions and not listening to what is being discussed.

Remember, some of the discussion questions have more than one answer, or there is no "right" answer. Children may voice a completely different response than expected.

Activities

Where in the World Was I Born?

✓ **SUPPLIES**

World map (attached to a wall)

Pushpins (one per child)

Small labels or paper pennants made of construction paper
(one per child)

Pencils or pens

A week prior to this session, have the children ask their parents about their place of birth. An adopted child may voice a concern that his exact birthplace is not known. Utilizing the city of adoption is an easy solution.

The adult moderator cuts tiny pennants, no longer than two inches, from construction paper. Write the children's names, one on each pennant. Tape the pennants to the plastic part of the pushpins. The moderator should make one for him- or herself as well.

It is suggested that the children go to the map one at a time to add their pennants. To keep a lively pace, assist individuals in locating their place of birth as needed. As the child steps forward, he could say, "Where in the world was I born?" and then tell the city or town, state or province, or country—depending upon the level of awareness that he has about geography.

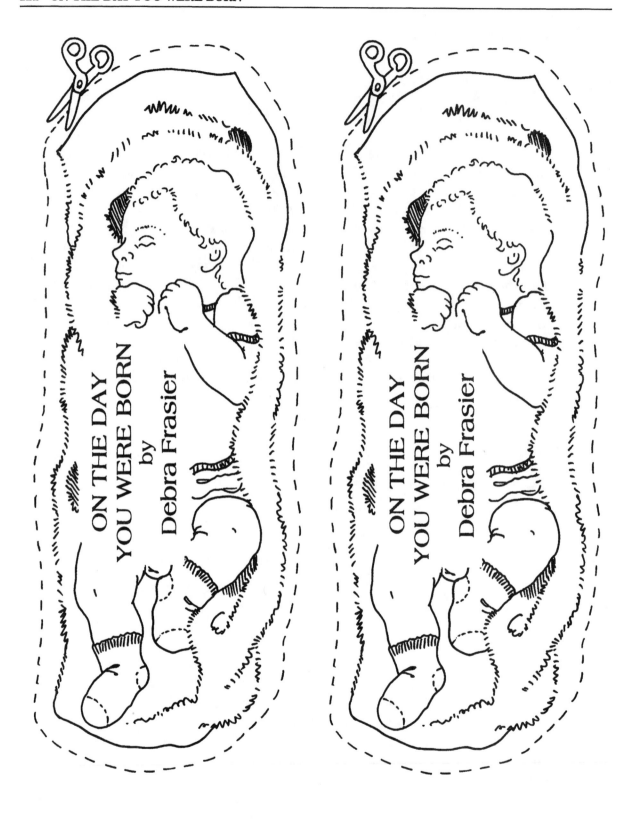

Figure 9.2. Baby for Discussion Questions

Discussion Questions

Why is it important to celebrate birthdays, marriages, and graduations?	What do you think a "family tree" is?
What gift would you give to the planet Earth?	What birthday present would you give to your best friend?
Look at the dedication page. Discuss the "honorees" listed there.	Read Debra Frasier's note found at the bottom of the verso page. What does this information tell you about the author's beliefs?
Does your family have birthday traditions that they follow?	Do you know why your parents gave you your name? If so, tell the group.
Look at the front and back covers of the book. Describe what you see.	In what season of the year were you born?
What is your favorite season? Why?	Do you resemble anyone in your family?
How could the arrival of a new baby change a family?	How might the arrival of one small baby affect the world?
Which page of collage art is your favorite?	Describe the best birthday celebration you have ever had.

Happy Birthday to Me! Game

Figure 9.3. Birthday Cake Sketch

✓ **SUPPLIES**

Two different bright colors of copy or construction paper for each child

One die for every six players

Scissors

There are two pages of patterns for the Happy Birthday to Me! game (Figures 9.4A–F, pages 125–26). To make the playing pieces more colorful, photocopy each of the two pages on a different color of construction paper. Each player will need to have a seven-piece pattern set: a plate, two cake layers, icing, candle, and two flowerettes. If possible, laminate the pattern pages before cutting.

Divide the players into groups of no more than six. Distribute the game pieces and give a single die to each group. Before beginning the game, the players must determine their own "lucky" numbers by a roll of the die. No one may have the same number.

The players begin with the plate pieces in front of them. The individual who has rolled lucky number one begins the game. Each turn consists of only one roll of the die. If the child rolls his or her lucky number, then one piece of the birthday cake is selected; thus begins the building of that player's cake.

If a number other than the lucky number is rolled, the player passes the die on to the next person and no piece is added. The first person in each group to complete a cake calls out, "Happy birthday to me!" The rest of the group sings the "Happy Birthday to You" song with much enthusiasm.

Once a player finishes a cake, he or she is no longer in the game. The player will give his or her lucky number to someone else in the group. Who gets the lucky number is the player's choice. The play resumes until all in the group have completed birthday cakes. See Figure 9.3 for an example of a completed birthday cake.

Note: After the first couple of players have finished their cakes, the game will proceed quickly because players will have more than one lucky number.

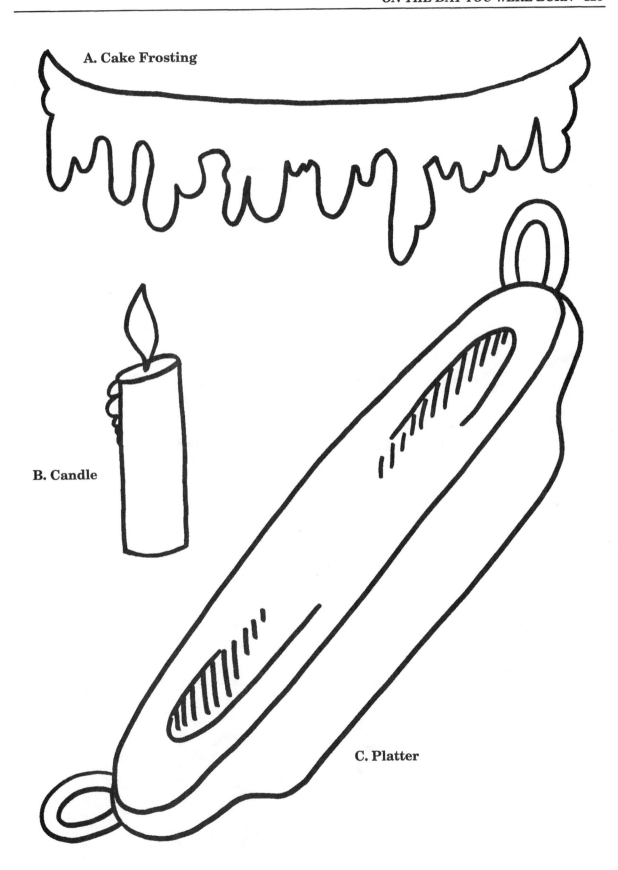

A. Cake Frosting

B. Candle

C. Platter

Figure 9.4. Birthday Cake Patterns

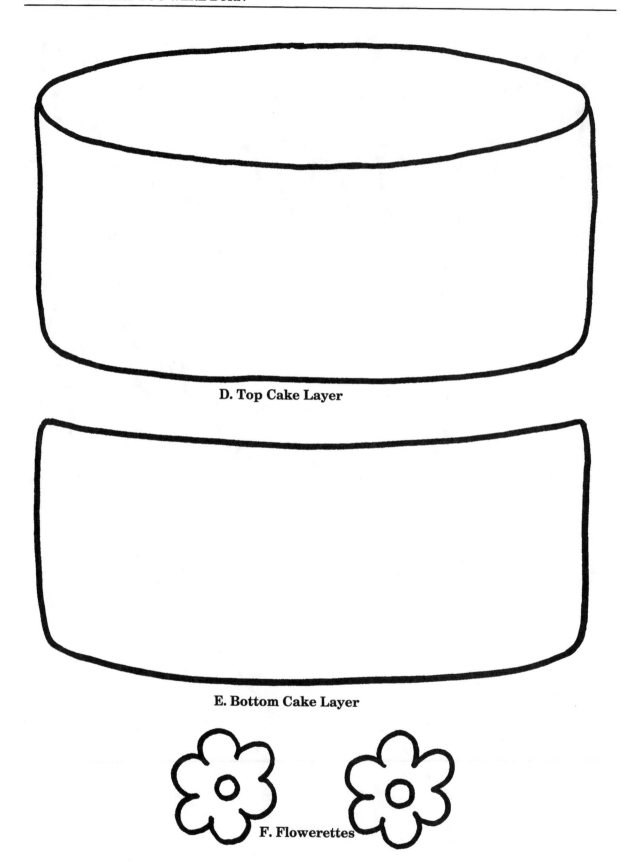

D. Top Cake Layer

E. Bottom Cake Layer

F. Flowerettes

Figure 9.4. Birthday Cake Patterns

Crafts

Leafy Family Tree Craft

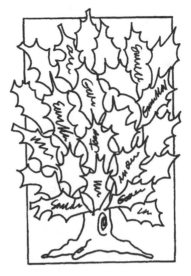

Figure 9.5. Leafy Family Tree Sketch

✓ **SUPPLIES**

> 11-by-17-inch (or larger) white construction paper
>
> Green and brown (or tan) construction paper
>
> Scissors
>
> Markers or crayons
>
> Glue sticks
>
> Scrap or notebook paper for listing names

Transfer the patterns (Figures 9.6A and B, page 128) onto poster board or cardboard and cut them out. These will be templates for the children to use. If time is a factor, cut out a tree trunk and a dozen or so leaves for each child. If time is not a factor, allow the children to trace around the templates and cut out their own trunks and leaves.

Distribute the white, 11-by-17-inch background paper. Have the children label their papers with the heading "My Family Tree" at the top edge of an 11-inch side. Glue the tree trunk as low as possible at the bottom edge to allow lots of room for the leaves. (See Figure 9.5 for an illustration of the completed craft.)

Children may now start making a practice list of their immediate family members plus other relatives, such as grandparents, uncles, aunts, and cousins. Emphasize to the children that if they are unsure of the correct spelling of a family member's name to wait until they get home to put the name permanently on the leaf.

Some children will be cognizant of extended family members and some will not. Family members can enjoy together this "under construction" project.

Note: Depending upon the age of the child, it may not be as important to define a father's and mother's side of the family as it would be to see that all relatives are represented on the family tree.

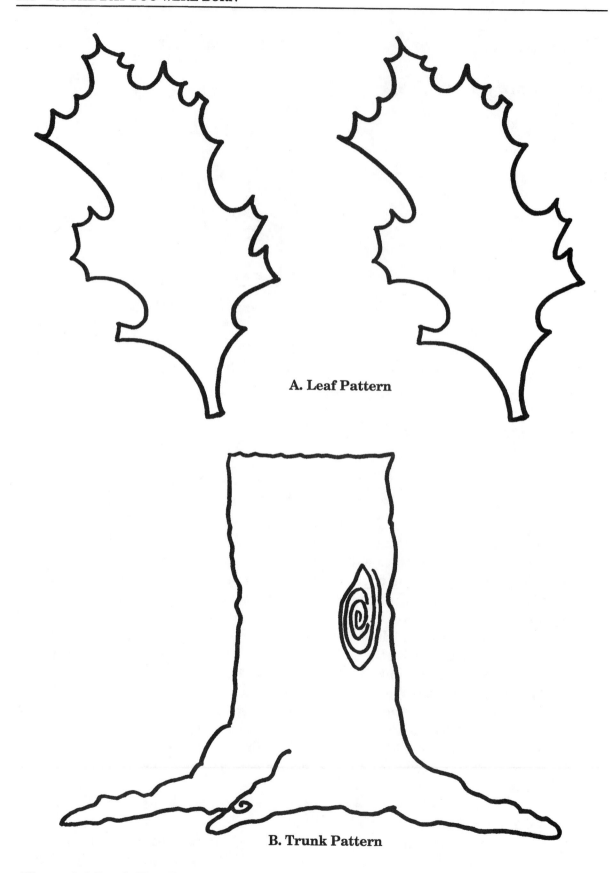

A. Leaf Pattern

B. Trunk Pattern

Figure 9.6. Leafy Family Tree Patterns

"On the Day I Was Born . . ." Booklet

✓ **SUPPLIES**

White or light-colored copy paper

Paper cutter or scissors

Single-hole punch

Stapler

Photocopy a set of pages for each child in the book club (Figures 9.7A–C, pages 130–32), and cut along the lines to create the pages for the booklet. There will be eight pages, including a cover and a blank page for additional ideas. Bind each booklet together with a single staple at the upper right-hand corner. Other than the cover, the order of pages is irrelevant.

Family input will be needed for this project. Send the booklets home a week before sharing *On the Day You Were Born*. Ask the children to talk with their parents, grandparents, or other relatives regarding the statements in the booklet, and have them collect and note their answers for each page. For example, "On the Day I Was Born . . . The Season Was _____." The child will ask a relative in what season (spring, summer, fall, or winter) was he/she born. Some children may want to insert additional pages for their own questions.

There are no wrong answers and some pages may remain blank. Children, however, will want to share their booklets with the other young readers. Prepare for this to be a memorable experience for all involved.

Assure the children that they and their family members will have lots of fun and laughs with this project. Announce that sharing will be encouraged but not mandated. Provide crayons and markers for the children to decorate their booklets during the book club session.

Snacks

Anything that suggests a party or celebration might be served, from the most simple candy treats to a full-sized cake with candles. If time allows, decorate the area around the serving table with birthday party items, such as crepe streamers, birthday-theme paper tablecloth, napkins, paper plates, and cups. Create a "Happy Birthday to All of Us" sign to tape on the wall.

Jelly beans

Punch or fruit juice

Cupcakes or muffins

Ice cream

ON THE DAY I WAS BORN

by

_____

On the Day I Was Born...

I was given my name because...

_____

_____

_____

On the Day I Was Born...

The season was _____

and

The weather was _____

Figure 9.7A. On the Day I Was Born Booklet Patterns

On the Day I Was Born...

Something funny, exciting, or
    unusual happened (choose one):

_____

On the Day I Was Born...

The date was_____

The time was_____

The place was_____

My weight was_____

My length was_____

On the Day I Was Born...

My mother said_____

_____

                and

My father said_____

_____

Figure 9.7B. On the Day I Was Born Booklet Patterns

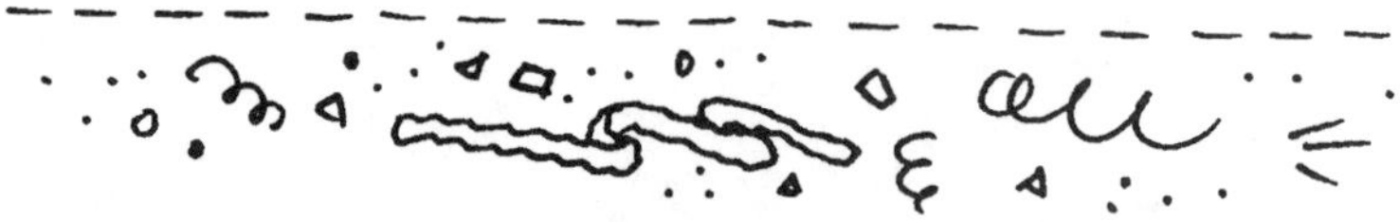

On the Day I Was Born...

My mother did this:_____

_____

and

My father did this:_____

_____

Figure 9.7C. On the Day I Was Born Booklet Patterns

Other Titles to Share

Arnold, Caroline. *Everybody Has a Birthday*. Illustrated by Anthony Accardo. New York: Franklin Watts, 1987. [33 pages]

Informational text explains celebrations, traditions, icons, and even superstitions associated with birthdays.

Bruchac, Joseph, and Jonathan London. *Thirteen Moons on a Turtles Back: A Native American Year of Moons*. Illustrated by Thomas Locker. New York: Philomel, 1992. [31 pages]

A collection of poems presents Native American myths that relate the wonder of the seasons and the thirteen moons of the year.

Clifton, Lucille. *Everett Anderson's Nine Month Long*. Illustrated by Ann Grifalconi. New York: Henry Holt, 1978. [26 pages]

A young boy's family changes over the nine months of his mother's pregnancy.

Curtis, Jamie Lee. *Tell Me Again About the Night I Was Born*. Illustrated by Laura Cornell. New York: HarperCollins, 1996. [29 pages]

A child asks yet again to be told the story of the night she was born, how her adoptive parents came for her, and how a family was immediately created.

Ehlert, Lois. *Red Leaf, Yellow Leaf*. San Diego: Harcourt Brace Jovanovich, 1991. [34 pages]

Burlap, ribbon, wire, seeds, and paper are used to create the story of a child's dear friend—a sugar maple tree.

Erlback, Arlene. *Happy Birthday, Everywhere!* Illustrated by Sharon Lane Holm. Brookfield, CT: Millbrook Press, 1997. [48 pages]

Unique presentation of birthday customs, foods, crafts, games, and languages for nineteen countries.

Feldman, Eve B. *Birthdays! Celebrating Life Around the World*. Mahwah, NJ: Bridgewater Books, 1996. [32 pages]

Illustrations from children of twenty-seven countries show how birthdays are celebrated around the world.

Horton, Barbara Savadge. *What Comes in Spring?* Illustrated by Ed Young. New York: Alfred A. Knopf, 1992. [28 pages]

Using the seasons of the year to set a beautiful time frame, a mother shares with her daughter the story of how the child grew inside her.

Katz, Karen. *Over the Moon: An Adoption Tale*. New York: Henry Holt, 1997. [26 pages]

The author's personal story of how she and her husband traveled to Central America to adopt their daughter.

Martin, Bill, and John Archambault. *Knots on a Counting Rope*. Illustrated by Ted Rand. New York: Henry Holt, 1987. [31 pages]

A Native American boy and his grandfather share the memories of the birth night and other special events of the child's life. With each "telling" another knot is tied in the counting rope.

Notes Alive! On the Day You Were Born. Narrated by Debra Frasier. Music by Steve Heitzeg. 30 min. Minneapolis: Minnesota Orchestral Association, 1996. Videocassette.

Frasier's picture book becomes a story concert. Frasier and Heitzeg, composer of original music, discuss the artistic creation of both book and symphony. A 1997 Notable Children's Video by the American Library Association / Association for Library Service to Children.

Notes Alive! Based on *On the Day You Were Born* by Debra Frasier. Creative Arts Enrichment Curriculum. Featuring the Minnesota Orchestra with music by Steve Heitzeg and conducted by William Eddins.

This kit contains curriculum guide, reproducible lessons, hardcover picture book, video with 3-D animation, music CD, and poster. Call 1-888-MN-NOTES or 612-371-7123 to order.

Yolen, Jane. *Ring of Earth: A Child's Book of Seasons*. Illustrated by John Wallner. San Diego: Harcourt Brace Jovanovich, 1986. [32 pages]

The seasons and four animals are intertwined through insightful poetry and lush, watercolor illustration.

Contacting the Publisher

Contact the marketing department at Harcourt Inc. at 525 B Street, Suite 1900, San Diego, CA 92101-4495, 619-699-6716, http://www.harcourtbooks.com. Ask what promotional items they have for *On the Day You Were Born*, such as posters, bookmarks, and the author's biography. Request enough supplies for each child in your book club and your files.

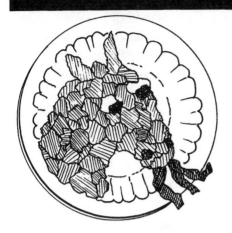

CHAPTER 10

The Paper Bag Princess

By Robert Munsch

Illustrated by Michael Martchenko

Munsch, Robert. *The Paper Bag Princess*. Illustrated by Michael Martchenko. Toronto, ON, Canada: Annick Press, 1995, 1980. [30 pages]

> *Princess Elizabeth saves Prince Ronald from the dragon only to discover that her attire is inappropriate.*

Introduction

Everyone enjoys the exciting tales of brave knights who slay dragons and save kingdoms. *St. George and the Dragon*, retold by Margaret Hodges and *Dove Isabeau* by Jane Yolen are two outstanding examples. (See "Other Titles to Share" in this chapter.) *The Paper Bag Princess* provides a humorous twist on the traditional version. Princess Elizabeth uses her wits, instead of force, to defeat the dragon and save her beloved Prince Ronald.

When children read books like *The Paper Bag Princess,* they wonder what it would have been like to live during the medieval time period. All sorts of questions come to mind: How heavy is a suit of armor? Would I want to live in a castle? What kinds of food would I eat? What types of dress, shirts, and hats would I wear? What games could I play?

The word "medieval" comes from the Latin medium aevum, which means "middle ages." This time period covered roughly a thousand years from the fifth century to the fifteen century.

The nobility wore clothing made from expensive fabrics such as silk and velvet. Feathers, fur, and ribbons adorned their brightly colored wardrobes. Jewelry made from precious stones and gold adorned their fingers and clothing. It is no wonder that snobby Prince Ronald was shocked by Princess Elizabeth's plain, paper sack.

Those who lived at court with the royal family enjoyed rich and varied lives. Monarchs liked to display their wealth and power by furnishing their castles with intricate tapestries, gold-painted furniture, and brilliant mosaics. There were many banquets with sumptuous and elaborate foods such as roasted peacocks and swans. People enjoyed hunts and tournaments, plus music and entertainment from actors, troubadours, and court jesters. They played games such as chess, backgammon, and cards.

Sharing *The Paper Bag Princess* can be very enjoyable because a lot of information on medieval life is available. Books about knights, castles, and royalty abound. In addition to discussing court life during this time period, the book by Robert Munsch and Michael Martchenko also offers the opportunity for deeper discussions. What did Princess Elizabeth do when tragedy struck? And how did she handle her problem (the dragon)?

Begin the session by playing the Hide the Ring Game (page 143) using, of course, one of Princess Elizabeth's royal rings. Follow this by serving snacks similar to those served at a medieval feast. Introduce the author and illustrator and conduct a discussion session. End with either the Paper Bag Shirt craft (page 143) or the Torn Paper Dragon craft (page 144). The Dragon Picture Poetry (page 141) can be completed as an extending activity for the classroom or as a take-home project. Have the children bring their poetry to the following book club meeting to display in the library or classroom.

Introducing the Author and Illustrator

Robert Munsch

Used by permission of Robert Munsch.

As a young man, Robert Munsch did not know what he wanted to do in life. He began working part-time at an orphanage and found that he liked being around children.

"I decided to work in day care for a year until I figured out what I wanted to do," writes Munsch, in the autobiography on his Web site. "And what I figured out I wanted to do was to work in day care."

Munsch went back to school at the Elliot Pearson School of Child Studies at Tufts University in Medford, Massachusetts. During his student teaching he created his first story, *Mortimer* (Annick Press, 1985). Other stories followed and he began to tell many prince and princess stories. Out of that came *The Paper Bag Princess*.

"I first told it (*The Paper Bag Princess*) in 1973 at the Bay Area Childcare Centre," says Munsch. "It was seven years old when it was published."

The smart and brave Princess Elizabeth is based upon his wife, and it was his wife who inspired the unique ending. "My wife Ann, who worked at the same Centre, suggested I try a reverse ending as she was tired of regular 'princess' endings."

The Munsch family moved to Canada and worked at the University of Guelph's lab preschool. A children's librarian heard Munsch tell his stories and encouraged him to write them down and send them to a publisher. He did not listen at first, but eventually did. *The Paper Bag Princess* was his third book to be published. It sold so well that Munsch quit his job at the lab preschool and began a full-time job of writing and telling stories.

When asked what he enjoys best about being a writer and a storyteller, Munsch replies, "Telling and traveling and writing and visiting families and mail and e-mail. I like the mix of things."

Munsch was born June 11, 1945, in Pittsburgh, Pennsylvania. He is one of nine children. When his siblings were not teasing him, Munsch liked to daydream and write poetry. Today, this best-selling author enjoys walking his dog, reading, writing, and dropping in unexpectedly on schools and day cares to tell stories. Before traveling to a city, Munsch likes to look in his files to see if any schools from that city have written him a letter. If time allows, he knocks on the classroom door and announces, "Hi! I'm Bob Munsch. Remember you asked me to come and visit when you wrote me last year?"

Robert Munsch can be contacted at 15 Sharon Place, Guelph, ON N1H 7V2, Canada.

Michael Martchenko

Photo courtesy of Annick Press Ltd., Toronto, Canada.

Michael Martchenko left France, with his family, when he was seven years old and moved to Ontario, Canada. "I went to school, where they only spoke English, but they presented me with a box of crayons," says Martchenko. "I couldn't believe it—this was for me?! One day I broke the end off of one and it scared me to death. I thought they were going to take the crayons away from me."

Martchenko always knew that he wanted to be an illustrator. As far back as he can remember he would sit and scribble. In high school he did cartoons of Macbeth and Hamlet, in addition to his own creations.

The Paper Bag Princess was Martchenko's first children's book project. "I got into children's book illustration by accident," says Martchenko. "I entered one of my whimsical pieces in an art show. [Robert] Munsch and an Annick Press representative spotted my work and called the next day.

"I always liked cartooning and humor. I thought it [*The Paper Bag Princess*] was a funny story, and different for its time."

Princess Elizabeth spends ninety-nine percent of the story in a paper bag, so Martchenko designed her with skinny arms and legs, haystack hair, and a melted, charred crown. His favorite illustration is on the cover—Princess Elizabeth meets the dragon at the entrance of his cave.

In designing the dragon, Martchenko worked for the right expression. "I didn't want the dragon to be fierce," says Martchenko. "He's kind of a goof, but a dangerous goof."

When visiting with children at schools, Martchenko is often asked if he could always draw well. "Of course not," says Martchenko. "I worked hard at it and kept improving. To be given a talent and waste it is a terrible thing. Anyone who is interested in art and thinks they are not very good, I tell them, 'Of course you are not very good. You are only six years old.' "

Michael Martchenko was born August 1, 1942, in Carcassone, France. He is married to Patricia Kerr and they have three daughters: Holly Michelle, Susan, and Janet. He can be contacted at 100 Airdrie Road, Toronto, ON M4G 1M3, Canada.

Discussion Questions

Make sixteen photocopies of the dragon graphic (Figure 10.1) on green paper. Reproduce the questions (page 140) on white paper. Cut and glue them to the back of the dragons. Laminate, if possible, and cut along the outlines of the dragons.

Pass the discussion questions around in a small basket. For an added touch, make a crown using yellow construction paper and tape it around a circular basket or plastic bowl. The dragons should be face up with the questions hidden from view.

Have one child select a dragon, read the question aloud, and give his or her opinion or answer. If desired, the discussion can be opened to the group for others to give their viewpoints or thoughts. Then the child passes the basket to the next individual who repeats the process. Allow only one dragon to be drawn at a time. This prevents others from reading and concentrating on their questions and not listening to what is being discussed.

Remember, some of the discussion questions have more than one answer, or there is no "right" answer. Children may voice a completely different response than expected.

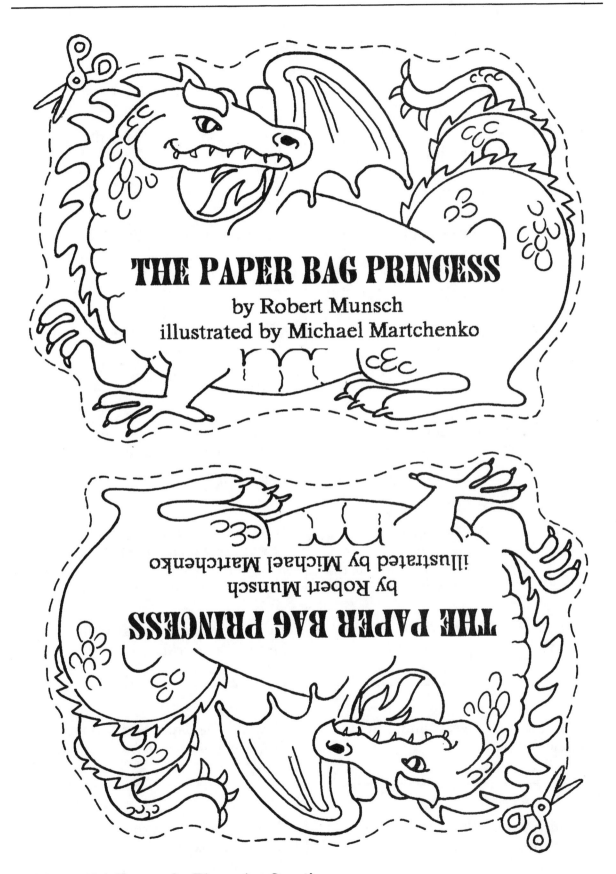

THE PAPER BAG PRINCESS
by Robert Munsch
illustrated by Michael Martchenko

Figure 10.1. Dragon for Discussion Questions

Discussion Questions

What happened when the dragon arrived at Elizabeth's castle?	How did Elizabeth track the dragon?
Which is your favorite illustration?	Describe Princess Elizabeth.
Describe Prince Ronald.	What weapon does Elizabeth use to defeat the dragon?
Who is a brave person that you know?	What did Ronald say when Elizabeth rescued him?
Why did Elizabeth decide not to marry Ronald?	How many forests could the dragon burn in one huge breath?
Would Ronald make a good friend? Why?	How fast could the dragon fly around the world?
What is the bravest thing you have done?	How did the paper bag survive the dragon's fiery breath?
Which part of the story is your favorite?	What do you think the dragon did when he woke up?

Activities

Dragon Picture Poetry Activity Sheet

Figure 10.2. Dragon Picture Poetry Example

Reproduce and give each book club participant a Dragon Picture Poetry activity sheet (Figure 10.3, page 142). Ask the children to think of words to describe a dragon; for example, "fiery," "sharp talons," or "steals princes." Have them create their own picture poetry by writing words or phrases to describe their dragons inside the patterns. Show them Figure 10.2 as an example of how they may want to write their own picture poetry.

DRAGON PICTURE POETRY

Create a different kind of poem—a picture poem.
Think of words to describe a dragon: fiery breath, shiny scales, burns castles.
Write those words anywhere you like inside the dragon—along the lines, inside the tummy, upside-down. Have fun and be creative.

Figure 10.3. Dragon Picture Poetry Activity Sheet

Hide the Ring Game

✓ **SUPPLIES**

Yarn (2 feet per player)

A fancy costume jewelry ring

Members of royalty were known for their beautiful rings, necklaces, pins, and crowns. Tell the group that they are going to play a game using one of Princess Elizabeth's royal rings.

Allow two feet of yarn per player. If there are fifteen players, cut thirty feet of yarn. Pass one end of the yarn through the ring and then tie the two ends together. All but one of the children take hold of a section of yarn in front of them and stand in a circle facing inward.

The remaining child stands in the center of the circle and closes her eyes. To start the game, the adult moderator chooses one of the children holding onto the yarn circle to hide the ring in his or her hand. Once the ring is hidden, the child in the center opens her eyes and tries to guess who has the hidden ring. The children secretly pass the ring from one person to another by sliding it along the yarn. When the person in the center correctly guesses which player has the ring, the two will trade places.

To make it difficult for the center person to guess who has the ring, all the children may want to move their hands back and forth on the yarn.

Crafts

Paper Bag Shirt Craft

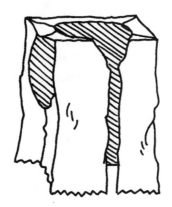

Figure 10.4. Paper Bag Shirt Sketch

✓ **SUPPLIES**

Large paper grocery bags (one per child)

Crayons or nonpermanent markers

Scissors

Optional: glue, fabric scraps, yarn, rickrack, buttons, glitter, and so forth.

Princess Elizabeth had to clothe herself in the only item not burned by the dragon's fiery breath—a paper bag. Perhaps if she had not been in such a hurry to rescue Prince Ronald, she would have taken time to decorate her makeshift outfit. With this craft, children will be able to create a paper bag shirt (or dress) worthy of royalty.

The paper bag shirts can be cut ahead of time, or the children can cut out the neck and armhole openings themselves. A plain side, with no grocery store advertising, is preferable as the front of the shirt. Cut an opening in the front of the bag, up the middle, from the bottom to the top. Continue by cutting a circle, at the base of the bag, for the head and neck. The bag should rest comfortably on the child's shoulders. Next cut an opening for each arm. Refer to Figure 10.4 as an example.

Optional: Give the children crayons, nonpermanent markers, glue, yarn, rickrack, scraps of fabric, buttons, and glitter to decorate their royal garments.

Torn Paper Dragon Craft

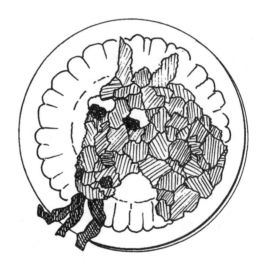

Figure 10.5. Torn Paper Dragon Sketch

✓ **SUPPLIES**

Sturdy paper plates (one per child)

Construction paper scraps

Tissue paper scraps

Glue

Single-hole punch

Yarn

Children may create either a picture of a dragon's face or of an entire dragon using torn paper art. Prepare an example to show the children.

Give the children scraps of construction paper and tissue paper in a variety of colors. Ask them to imagine a dragon. If they need assistance picturing what dragons look like, have books with illustrations of the imaginary creatures for review.

To create their dragon, they will tear paper into different shapes and sizes. For example, a child may tear pieces of yellow paper to create the face, red and orange paper to create fire coming from the mouth, and more red paper to design fiery eyes.

Glue the torn paper pieces into place on the paper plate. When finished, punch two holes at the top. Tie each end of an eight-inch piece of yarn into each of the two holes. The torn-paper dragons can be hung on a wall at the library or at home.

Snacks

Pita bread (or other flat bread)

Cheeses (American, Colby, Jack, etc.)

Fruit (apples, grapes)

Cookies

Introduce Aliki's *Medieval Feast* (see "Other Titles to Share" in this chapter) while the group enjoys a medieval snack of flat bread, cheeses, fruit, and cookies.

As described in Aliki's book, children will use the pita bread (or some other type of flat bread) as their plate. Cheeses and fruit can be placed on their "plates" and eaten. Cookies make an easy substitute for the pastries.

Other Titles to Share

Albee, Sarah. *The Dragon's Scales*. Illustrated by John Manders. New York: Random House, 1998. [48 pages]

Holly must use logic and math skills to outsmart a greedy dragon.

Aliki. *A Medieval Feast*. New York: Thomas Y. Crowell, 1983. [32 pages]

The lord and lady of the manor prepare a feast to welcome the visiting king and queen.

Hart, Avery, and Paul Mantell. *Knights & Castles: 50 Hands-on Activities to Experience the Middle Ages*. Illustrated by Michael Kline. Charlotte, VT: Williamson, 1998. [96 pages]

This book contains information and projects for an extended unit on the Middle Ages.

Hodges, Margaret. *St. George and the Dragon*. Illustrated by Trina Schart Hyman. Boston: Little, Brown, 1984. [32 pages]

Princess Una brings the Red Cross Knight to slay the dragon that holds her kingdom hostage.

Kleven, Elisa. *The Paper Princess*. New York: Dutton Children's Books, 1994. [32 pages]

A young girl draws and cuts a princess from paper and plays with her until the wind carries the princess away. The paper princess has many adventures as she tries to find her way back to the young girl.

Lewis, J. Patrick. *Night of the Goat Children*. Illustrated by Alexi Natchev. New York: Dial Books for Young Readers, 1999. [32 pages]

Birgitta the Brave cleverly saves her kingdom from outlaws by having five children dress as goats. Based upon a true story.

Martin, C. L. G. *The Dragon Nanny*. Illustrated by Robert Rayevsky. New York: Macmillan, 1988. [32 pages]

No longer employed by the King, Nanny Nell Hannah finds herself nanny to Sparky and Cinder, two baby dragons.

O'Brien, Patrick. *The Making of a Knight: How Sir James Earned His Armor*. Watertown, MA: Charlesbridge, 1998. [32 pages]

Factual information about becoming a knight is included in the story of young James growing up to serve Lord Hawkes.

Oram, Hiawyn. *The Second Princess*. Illustrated by Tony Ross. Racine, WI: Western, 1994. [26 pages]

Second Princess does not like being second and tries to find a way to get rid of First Princess.

Osborne, Mary Pope. *Molly and the Prince*. Illustrated by Elizabeth Sayles. New York: Alfred A. Knopf, 1994. [32 pages]

Molly discovers that an old, stray dog is not what he seems.

Scieszka, Jon. *The Frog Prince, Continued*. Illustrated by Steve Johnson. New York: Viking Penguin, 1991. [32 pages]

The Frog Prince goes in search of a witch to turn him back into a frog.

Sutcliff, Rosemary. *The Minstrel and the Dragon Pup*. Illustrated by Emma Chichester Clark. Cambridge, MA: Candlewick Press, 1993. [42 pages]

A traveling minstrel finds a dragon egg and raises the young creature. One night the animal is stolen and the minstrel goes on a quest to find his friend.

Wilsdorf, Anne. *Princess*. New York: Greenwillow Books, 1993. [32 pages]

This tale presents a delightful twist to the traditional princess and the pea story.

Yolen, Jane. *Dove Isabeau*. Illustrated by Dennis Nolan. San Diego: Harcourt Brace Jovanovich, 1989. [32 pages]

Dove Isabeau's evil stepmother turns her into a dragon. This forces Dove Isabeau to fight all the brave young men who come to slay the wyrm.

Contacting the Publisher

Contact the marketing department at Annick Press, 15 Patricia Avenue, Toronto, ON M2M 1H9 Canada, 416-221-4802, http://www.annickpress.com. Ask what promotional items they have for *The Paper Bag Princess*, such as posters, bookmarks, and the author's and illustrator's biographies. Request enough supplies for each child in your book club and your files.

CHAPTER 11

Buffalo Thunder

By Patricia Wittmann

Illustrated by Bert Dodson

Wittmann, Patricia. *Buffalo Thunder*. Illustrated by Bert Dodson. New York: Marshall Cavendish, 1997. [32 pages]

> *Young Karl Isaac is on his way west with his family in their prairie schooner. There are new sights, adventures, wagon train friends, American Indians, and hardships. Karl Isaac wants more—to see the wild buffalo! Illuminating artwork and an unforgettable frontier life story bring this picture book to life.*

Introduction

Who were the American pioneers of the 1800s that traveled westward on the perilous Oregon Trail? They were brave people; trailblazers who risked danger to travel across half a continent to a new, green land called Oregon. In their Conestoga wagons, often called prairie schooners, they stuffed everything a family would need for the journey: clothes, food, tools, and supplies. If space allowed, rocking chairs and iron cook stoves were brought along for the new log cabin to be built.

Oxen pulled the wagons. They were stronger than horses but slower. Consequently, the 2,000-mile trip would take at least six months. Only a few forts or trading outposts dotted the trail that traversed deserts, rivers, woods, prairies, and mountains. All kinds of weather conditions had to be endured—extreme heat and cold alike. Many pioneers died of starvation; others froze to death in snowstorms. If they were lucky, a stampeding buffalo herd would not crush them under thundering hooves.

During the mid-1800s, 20 million to 30 million American bison lived on the plains. Karl Isaac would have been sad to know that by 1889, because of the slaughter by hide hunters, less than 600 buffalo would remain alive.

149

A week prior to this session, suggest that the children attend wearing either a cowboy hat or a sunbonnet. In addition, ask that they bring an old-fashioned item, such as a horseshoe, a black-and-white family picture, or a quilt, to share with the group.

As the participants arrive, play some recorded fiddle or square dance music to set a lively mood. Serve refreshments and distribute the Karl Isaac's Dream Dot-to-Dot (Figure 11.2).

Play an exciting game of Chips in the Buffalo Wallow (pages 156–57) next or opt for writing with a quill pen (page 156); or, consider directing the group in a bit of square dancing. Then introduce author Patricia Wittmann and illustrator Bert Dodson by sharing the biographical information provided. Discussion questions might be passed around in a small, black skillet or miniature pail to help emphasize the theme.

If you choose, snacks can wait until after the activities and discussion. This will allow children to make butter in a jar. *Buffalo Thunder* describes butter being churned along the bumpy wagon trail. Children can pass a small jar of cream (see "Snacks") around the group so that all can take a turn shaking it. If you opt to do this activity, begin the butter at the start of the session. If you can, take twenty to thirty minutes for the butter to form. End with the craft, which is a freestanding buffalo made of poster board (pages 158–59).

Introducing the Author and Illustrator

Patricia Wittmann

Photo by Michael Van Horn.

"I have always been interested in history, and in the astounding things people did in the past," states Patricia Wittmann. "Four generations ago, my relatives came west on the Oregon Trail. My family still has a rocking chair and a coffee grinder that was brought on their wagon. It's really something to think that they literally *walked* across the United States—2,000 miles! And why did they walk? Because the wagon was too full of all of their belongings for them to ride."

Perhaps it was inevitable that Wittmann would one day write about American pioneers. Her relatives were early settlers of Vancouver, Washington, and most of her large family has always lived in the Northwest.

At regional archival libraries, she studied numerous original journals and diaries written in the 1840s by travelers of the Oregon Trail. The Pacific Northwest, where she lives today, was considered the "end of the road;" therefore historical records, literature, and artifacts are abundant.

"Once they reached their destination, many pioneers no longer wrote in their journals and diaries because they were too busy building their new homes and working the land," explains Wittmann. "I've read some wonderful accounts written by the pioneers of the Oregon Trail. People wrote of hearing buffalo before they were even seen. They wrote about how the dust clouds built, and how the ground rumbled. They used beautiful language describing the vast prairie and their difficult journey across it. I read and read until I got a strong feeling for their experience."

As a young reader, Wittmann was "crazy about old-fashioned stories." She read the Little House on the Prairie series over and over again, and remembers *Caddie Woodlawn* as a favorite. The family basement had an entire wall of bookshelves filled with books, and Wittmann was an avid reader.

Young Wittmann's parents encouraged her to be an artist. In school, she earned her best grades in art and history, but confesses that she did not consider herself a good writer. Today she works as a food stylist for cookbooks and magazines, and has three other children's books to her credit: *Go Ask Giorgio!* (Simon & Schuster, 1992), *Scrabble Creek* (Macmillan, 1993), and *Clever Gretchen* (Cavendish, 2000), a folktale adapted by John Stewig.

Wittman enjoys visiting schools to talk about *Buffalo Thunder*, her love of history, and how her family played a part in the settling of the Northwest.

Address correspondence to Patricia Wittmann at 5823 First Avenue NW, Seattle, WA 98107.

Bert Dodson

Photo by Joe Mehling.

Dodson was born and raised in southwest Texas, so when he was asked to illustrate *Buffalo Thunder*, he had an existing mental image of cowboys, dust storms, and the plains. Although Dodson had never witnessed a stampeding buffalo herd, the consummate artist had few concerns. He has drawn and painted almost everything, from detailed medical illustrations to Western art, which includes more than sixty books for children.

"I have worked very hard for many, many years to develop and perfect my drawing and illustrating techniques, so, lots of job possibilities now come my way," says Dodson, from his studio and gallery in Bradford, Vermont. "I try to take time to share my knowledge with children who aspire to be artists. I know from experience the importance of encouragement."

When Dodson was a preschooler, his mother saw a blossoming talent. She showed family and friends pages from his coloring books. "She was my first champion," professes Dodson, "but when she showed me those coloring books after I was grown, I must admit that I thought the work looked like the typical scribbles of a five-year-old."

As a boy, the artist remembers that his favorite books were *Winnie the Pooh*, *The Jungle Book*, and the Beatrix Potter collection. "I scrutinized the drawings because I knew early on that I wanted art to be my life's work."

When Dodson develops illustrations for a historical fiction picture book, like *Buffalo Thunder*, he feels strongly that his first obligation is to support the author's story and to allow the reader to have a singular experience with the art and text. "This boy moving west with his family had to *look* like a boy of those times," says Dodson. "From the details on the Conestoga wagon to the pioneers' clothes to the tongues hanging out of the buffalos' mouths—all had to present an atmosphere of realism.

"An illustrator must be accurate, and that is the result of much research. I studied a series of books on the Conestoga wagon to learn how to draw them. And because there are no buffalo herds in Vermont, I watched hours and hours of movie videos so that I could draw and paint stampeding buffalo in a believable way."

Bert Dodson welcomes written correspondence at his home, which he shares with his dog and two cats. His address is Box 1660, Bradford, VT 05033.

Discussion Questions

Make sixteen photocopies of the buffalo on light brown or tan paper (Figure 11.1). Reproduce the questions (page 154) on white copy paper. Cut and glue them to the back of the buffaloes. Laminate, if possible, and cut along the outlines of the buffaloes.

Pass the discussion questions around in a small basket. The buffaloes should be face up with the questions hidden from view. Have one child select a buffalo from the basket, read the question aloud, and give his or her opinion or answer. If desired, the discussion can be opened to the group for others to give their viewpoints or thoughts. Then the child passes the basket to the next individual who repeats the process. Allow only one buffalo to be drawn at a time. This prevents others from reading and concentrating on their questions and not listening to what is being discussed.

Remember, some of the discussion questions have more than one answer, or there is no "right" answer. Children may voice a completely different response than expected.

Activities

Karl Isaac's Dream Dot-to-Dot

Photocopy the activity sheet (Figure 11.2, page 155) for each child in the book club.

Figure 11.1. Buffalo for Discussion Questions

Discussion Questions

To whom did the author dedicate her book? Do you think it may have influenced her writing *Buffalo Thunder*?	Do you live close to or far away from your grandparents or other relatives? How do you feel about that?
How would it feel to give away a pet because you were moving?	What feelings do you think Karl Isaac had after the buffalo herd was gone?
This story took place in 1845. What kinds of things were not yet invented?	Have you taken a long car trip? What did you do to ease boredom?
What would it have been like to travel in a covered wagon for months?	Describe the wildlife Karl Isaac would have seen on the Oregon Trail.
How would you make a campfire using buffalo chips?	How do the illustrations make the book enjoyable?
Look at the illustrations of the oxen and wagon. Why do you think there are no reins?	What is a buffalo wallow? Use a dictionary if you need help.
What did Karl Isaac do when he was scared? What do you do?	What did Karl Isaac eat every day? Would you get tired of eating hamburgers every day?
Name some toys or games that a pioneer child would have played on a journey westward.	What things would one see now on the road to Oregon that Karl Isaac would not have seen?

KARL ISAAC'S DREAM

Use your pencil to connect the dots from numbers 1 to 52 to see what young Karl Isaac dreamed about.

Figure 11.2. Karl Isaac's Dream Dot-to-Dot

Writing with Quill Pens

For this activity, provide children with quill pens, paper, bottles of washable ink, and a flat writing surface. If possible, show samples of fine quill penmanship. The children can write journal entries about what they did that day. Prior to the session, carefully cut away the tips of each quill shaft to make a sharp point. See Figure 11.3 below.

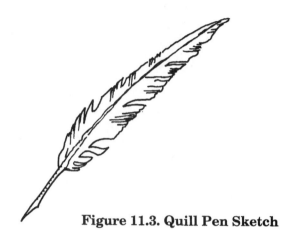

Figure 11.3. Quill Pen Sketch

✓ **SUPPLIES**

Large feathers (purchase at a hobby story)

Sharp craft knife (for adult use only)

Washable, bottled ink

Writing paper

Look at the illustration on the title page of *Buffalo Thunder*. Do you believe it is of Karl Isaac before or after his Oregon Trail journey? He is using a sharpened goose quill (large feather) as a writing instrument. Quill pens were still used by many in the 1800s because they were affordable. Dark berry juice was often the only ink available. Have fun trying your writing skills with a quill pen.

Chips in the Buffalo Wallow Game

There were no toy stores along the Oregon Trail in the 1800s. Families made toys from objects found in nature and played games that demanded little or no equipment. Imagine that Karl Isaac created his own game while collecting buffalo chips for a campfire. To entertain himself, Karl Isaac may have attempted to sail buffalo chips into a wallow. Buffaloes rolled their heavy bodies in the dirt to scratch their itchy skin. This rolling formed circular impressions in the ground called wallows.

Figure 11.4. Paper Plate Buffalo Chip

✓ **SUPPLIES**

6–10 small paper plates

Brown spray paint (for adult use only)

Cool glue gun (for adult use only)

White liquid glue or glue stick

Dried straw or grass

Hula hoop, masking tape, or chalk

Making Buffalo Chips

Because of the drying time involved, the adult moderator will make the "buffalo chips" at least one day prior to the actual session. The glue needs to dry thoroughly before the chips can be tossed during the game. Send instructions home with the children so that they can play with family and friends.

Make each buffalo chip by gluing two plates together. The inside (eating) surfaces will be glued facing each other. Using a cool glue gun, run a bead of glue around the edge of one plate and place the other plate on top. Press the edges firmly together.

Paint the top and bottom with the brown spray paint. Spread liquid glue on one surface at a time. Press grass or straw and bits of earth onto the sticky surface. Allow it to dry completely before using. (See Figure 11.4 for an illustration of the completed buffalo chip.)

Playing the Game

Designate the buffalo wallow with a hula hoop or a circle created with masking tape or chalk. Depending upon the age and abilities of the children in your group, mark a line for the participants to stand behind. Direct the children to sail two buffalo chips into the circle. (Throwing two buffalo chips determines one turn.) A point is given for each chip that lands fully inside the circle.

Craft

Bodacious Bison Craft

Figure 11.5. Bodacious Bison Sketch

✓ **SUPPLIES**

Brown poster board or tag board

Scissors

Nonpermanent markers or crayons

Cotton balls or fake fur (optional)

Brown spray paint (optional; for adult use only)

1-inch piece of yarn or macramé per child (optional)

Liquid glue

Children will create a freestanding bison by fitting three pattern pieces together (Figures 11.6A–C). Prior to the session, create templates from which the children will trace and cut their bison parts. Transfer the three pattern pieces (Figures 11.6A–C) to poster board. Cut enough patterns for the group to use.

Be sure to mark the dots on the templates and direct the children to copy the dots on their patterns. These markings will tell the children where to fit the pieces together.

After the children have traced and cut their three buffalo pattern pieces, they can add features such as ears, horns, and hooves. At the dots, slide the slots of the two leg pieces in place on the buffalo's underside. Adjust them so that the buffalo is freestanding.

To create the thick pelage around the animal's shoulders, glue into place small pieces of fur or cotton balls that have been sprayed brown. (Cut each cotton ball into quarters before spraying and gluing.) If desired, cut away the poster board tail and glue a one-inch piece of yarn or macramé. Encourage the children to finish both sides of their buffalo. (Refer to Figure 11.5 for an illustration of the completed craft.)

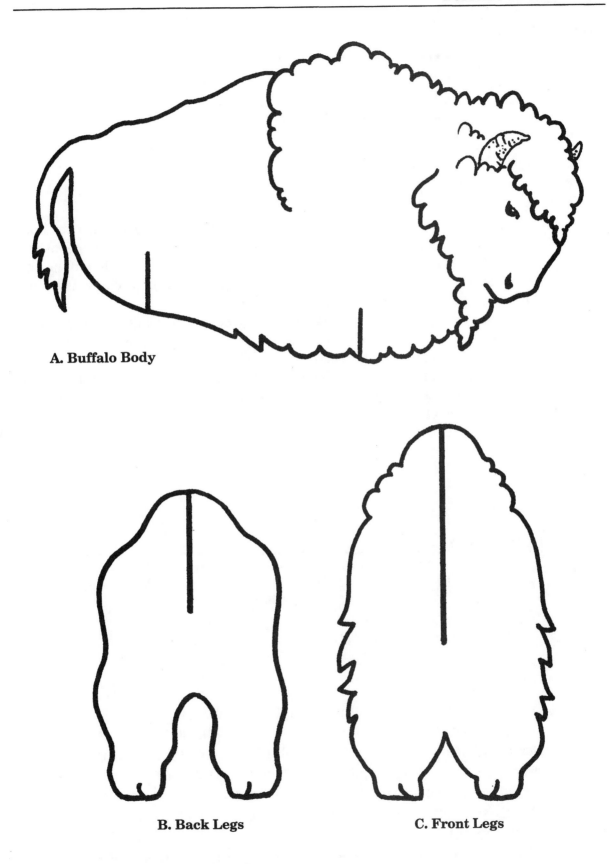

A. Buffalo Body

B. Back Legs

C. Front Legs

Figure 11.6. Bodacious Bison Patterns

Snacks

Cornbread

Pinto beans

Bumpy Trail butter

Beef jerky

Sarsaparilla (or root beer)

Request homemade cornbread and pinto beans from a cook with a generous nature. Canned varieties of pinto, Great Northern (white), or kidney beans will make this snack idea even easier. Use small paper cups or bowls plus plastic spoons for easy cleanup. If possible, provide washable quilts or blankets so that the children can sit on the floor as they eat.

There are numerous recipes for making beef jerky. This option will take pre-planning but it is a very easy process. Jerky is also available to purchase at most grocery stores, but can be expensive.

Unless a milk cow was available, most pioneers drank only water or coffee. Sarsaparilla (a plant whose fragrant roots were used as flavoring for a drink of the same name) could be represented by diluting root beer with water. Mix one part root beer to one part water. Bottled sarsaparilla may not be available for purchase in all areas.

Ma's Bumpy Trail Butter Recipe

INGREDIENTS

1 cup heavy whipping cream
1 drop yellow food coloring (optional)
Pinch of salt
Pint-sized glass jar with lid

DIRECTIONS

Pour the cream into the glass jar and allow it to warm to room temperature. Make sure the lid is on very tight, and begin shaking. Have children take turns shaking the jar for one to two minutes. After twenty to thirty minutes, a ball will begin to form as the cream thickens. Pour off the whey and drain the butter ball in paper towels. Gently squeeze the butter to remove any excess liquid. Serve on warm cornbread.

Other Titles to Share

Carlson, Laurie. *Boss of the Plains: The Hat That Won the West*. Illustrated by Holly Meade. New York: DK, 1998. [32 pages]

A picture book biography of John Batterson Stetson, the man who created the most popular hat of the west.

Coerr, Eleanor. *The Josefina Story Quilt*. Illustrated by Bruce Degen. New York: Harper & Row, 1986. [64 pages]

A young girl, with a pet hen named Josefina, works on a quilt as her family travels west in a covered wagon. Also available in audiobook.

Doner, Kim. *Buffalo Dreams*. Portland, OR: WestWinds Press, 1999. [38 pages]

An ancient Native American legend of the white buffalo is expanded in this modern family story with illustrations by the author. The legend of the White Buffalo Calf Woman and dreamcatcher craft directions are included.

Goble, Paul. *Iktomi and the Buffalo Skull: A Plains Indian Story*. New York: Orchard Books, 1991. [32 pages]

An amusing and interactive tale about trickster Iktomi and the need to respect the sacred buffalo skull.

Johnston, Marianne. *Buffaloes*. New York: Rosen Publishing Group, 1997. [24 pages]

Introduces the American bison to young readers, where and how it lives, plus brief historical facts. Includes clear color photographs.

Kalman, Bobbie. *The Wagon Train*. New York: Crabtree, 1999. [32 pages]

Depicts North American pioneers of the 1800s as they traveled west. This multifaceted work is appropriate for young readers because of the short entry format. A glossary and an index are included.

McClung, Robert M. *Shag: Last of the Plains Buffalo*. Illustrated by Louis Darling. Hamden, CT: Linnett Books, 1991. [96 pages]

This chapter book about an American bison from birth to death on the western plains provides a very insightful look at a buffalo's life struggles.

Moss, Marissa. *Rachel's Journal: The Story of a Pioneer Girl*. San Diego: Harcourt Brace, 1998. [48 pages]

Rachel writes and draws in her journal telling of her travels in a covered wagon across the Oregon Trail. This fictionalized account is presented in a handwritten journal with notes and sketches in the margins.

Roop, Peter, and Connie Roop. *Westward Ho! Ho! Ho!* Illustrated by Anne Canevari Green. Brookfield, CT: Millbrook Press, 1996. [40 pages]

A delightful collection of stories, riddles, jokes, and essays about the Oregon Trail, Native Americans, cowboys, and general frontier and pioneer life.

Stein, R. Conrad. *The Story of the Oregon Trail*. Illustrated by David Catrow. Chicago: Children's Press, 1984. [31 pages]

Engaging text of the people who traversed the Oregon Trail in the 1800s and the hardships they encountered.

Thomas, Joyce Carol. *I Have Heard of a Land*. Illustrated by Floyd Cooper. New York: HarperCollins, 1998. [32 pages]

Beautiful, poetic text of the experiences of an African American pioneer woman who, on her own, comes to the Oklahoma Territory to claim free land.

Webber, Desiree. *The Buffalo Train Ride*. Illustrated by Sandy Shropshire. Austin, TX: Eakin Press, 1999. [91 pages]

In 1907, efforts to reintroduce the buffalo to the midwestern plains begin with an exciting train journey that starts in New York and ends in the Oklahoma Territory. Historical photographs, maps, a glossary, and an index are included.

Wilder, Laura Ingalls. *Going West: Adapted from the Little House Books by Laura Ingalls Wilder*. Illustrated by Renée Graef. New York: HarperCollins, 1996. [32 pages]

A simple and satisfying story follows a pioneer family as they travel west in their covered wagon. Illustrated with bright watercolors.

Wilkinson, Todd. *Bison Magic for Kids*. Photographs by Michael H. Francis. Illustrated by John F. McGee. Milwaukee, WI: Gareth Stevens, 1995. [48 pages]

An informative and fun mixture of facts, great photos, and amusing drawings about the American buffalo make this a recommended title to read.

Wilson, Laura. *How I Survived the Oregon Trail: The Journal of Jesse Adams*. New York: Beech Tree Books, 1999. [38 pages]

Visually pleasing with photos of artifacts of the time, this book is a fictionalized journal of travel on the Oregon Trail during the 1800s. Games, recipes, and activities make this a very interactive read.

Contacting the Publisher

Contact the marketing department at Marshall Cavendish at 99 White Plains Road, P.O. Box 2001, Tarrytown, NY 10591-9001, 914-332-8888, http://www .marshallcavendish.com. Ask what promotional items they have for *Buffalo Thunder*, such as posters, bookmarks, and the author's and illustrator's biographies. Request enough supplies for each child in your book club and your files.

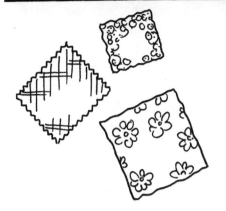

CHAPTER 12

The Rag Coat

By Lauren Mills

Mills, Lauren. *The Rag Coat*. New York: Little, Brown, 1991. [28 pages]

After the death of a father, a group of quilters create a winter coat from fabric scraps for the daughter. This is a warm, family story set in the Appalachian region.

Introduction

The Appalachian Mountains of eastern North America, stretching from Quebec, Canada, south to the state of Alabama, are the oldest mountains in the United States. After millions of years of rain, wind, and other weather extremes, they are worn smooth and sharp in contrast to the younger, jagged Rocky Mountains of the western United States.

Appalachia is the name given to the strikingly beautiful regions of the Appalachian Mountains where, even today, some residents live in poverty and isolation. It is an area rich in Scottish and Irish heritage, and where music, storytelling, and early American craft remain strong cultural influences.

As the session begins, play the musical recording of either Dolly Parton's or Emmy Lou Harris's version "Coat of Many Colors" (see "Other Titles to Share") to set the mood for the upcoming discussion and activities. Author Lauren Mills acknowledges that Harris's version, plus her own childhood experiences, influenced her creation of *The Rag Coat*.

In addition to Mills's title, share Dolly Parton's book *The Coat of Many Colors* (see "Other Titles to Share" in this chapter). Explain that Parton wrote her book, *The Coat of Many Colors,* from her song by the same title. It may also be fun to talk about other songs that have been transformed to a book format, such as those listed under "Other Titles to Share" in Chapter 15, "This Land Is Your Land."

When planning snacks, keep foods simple to emphasize the modest setting depicted in *The Rag Coat*. Children, like Minna, may have carried a cold biscuit and a glass jar of buttermilk to school for lunch in a small, tin box or bucket. Children might want to solve the Quilt Squares Secret Message (Figure 12.2) while they snack and listen to music.

To decorate the room for the program, consider displaying hand-sewn quilts. For an additional activity, play Hide the Thimble (page 170). Be sure to explain what a thimble is and how it is used. If possible, locate an individual with a thimble collection who would be willing to display it during the session. Share the biographical information on Lauren Mills, proceed with the discussion questions, and then end with the Pretty Paper Rag Coat craft on page 170. It will be surprising to all how many different coat styles are created from the same basic pattern. Be sure to have a fashion show so that the children can showcase their creations.

Introducing the Author/Illustrator

Lauren Mills

Dennis Nolan, Lauren Mills, and their daughter Evie.
Used by permission of Lauren Mills.

Lauren Mills admits that the people, the crafts, and the culture of Appalachia have always fascinated her. This region is the setting for her picture book, *The Rag Coat*. One may wonder if there is an autobiographical link to Minna, the main character, who proves to be resolute and forgiving when she is taunted and ostracized. Although Mills did not grow up in an Appalachian region, there does exist an intimate affiliation between the story line and her life experiences.

"Yes, there's a personal feeling of connection to the main character Minna," she says. "I remember being new to a school as a young person, and I was teased about a coat that I wore. It did have a quilted, patchwork look, and, possibly, as was Minna's, my coat was just different enough that the other kids felt they could make fun. It was a very difficult situation to deal with. It always is when you've moved to a new place and you haven't made friends yet.

"How painful it is to be teased or left out," she states. "I wanted to create a character that knew how to deal with it—a character that would not be mean in return—someone who would not retaliate.

"I would wish that the children and adults who read *The Rag Coat* would understand that we are all connected. We're all made of the same stuff . . . the same cloth. It's so important to be kind to one another."

Is Mills a seamstress like many of the characters in her book? "I love all crafts, but I am not a seamstress or even very good at sewing," she says. "I learned quilting, weaving, and dollmaking from my mother, grandmother, and aunt. I remember as a girl spending much of one summer with my aunt. We quilted a great deal. Those are fond memories."

Mills was an imaginative child. Although reading was not a favorite pastime, pretending to be historical and literary characters was. She spent many hours in the woods near her childhood home pretending to be Pocahontas. Mills did enjoy being read to; some of her favorites were *Snow White*, Francis Burnett's *The Little Princess*, and stories with animals. After reading time was over, though, she rushed outdoors. The adult Mills remembers that, when she was young, reading often gave her headaches and that she became nervous during test times at school. Today, however, reading is a favorite pastime.

Lauren Mills says there are parts of *The Rag Coat* that she favors. The illustration she likes best is the cameo of Minna on the title page, and her preferred passage is the father's statement, "People only need people, and nothing else." The author says she often thinks of these words when she observes people acting unkind to one another. Mills fondly suggests reading Eleanor Estes's *The Hundred Dresses* (see "Other Titles to Share" in this chapter). It, too, emphasizes the importance of good character over the importance of material possessions and explores the role of teasing.

The Rag Coat has been recognized in many ways as an outstanding book for children. It received the Charlotte Award, a New York State Reading Association Children's-Choice award. The University of Utah Children's Dance Theatre performed the story as a ballet, and many professional storytellers have asked Mills for permission to tell *The Rag Coat*.

Mills received her master's degree in book illustration from San Jose State University in California. She uses a variety of ways to create her art: sketching and painting people, using her imagination, and setting up nature still lifes indoors.

"I often bring in things from the outside, like branches and leaves, so that I can work on the tiny details. I also use live models. For example, I photographed, sketched, and painted people to create the individuals for *The Rag Coat*. The husband of Jane Dyer, who lives nearby and is a fellow children's book illustrator, was the model for Minna's father."

Mills says her favorite subject to illustrate is fairy folk, or little people. Examples of her work can be found in *Elfabet: An ABC of Elves* by Jane Yolen (Little, Brown, 1990, 1997), *The Goblin Baby* written and illustrated by Mills (Penguin Putnam, 1999), and *Fairy Wings* written and illustrated by Mills and her husband Dennis Nolan (Little, Brown, 1995). "In *Elfabet* I had to use my memory extensively to create the art. That book, you see, had numerous illustrations of fairy folk and, as everyone knows, fairies do not hold still for very long at all."

Mills lives in Massachusetts with her husband Dennis Nolan, who is also an author and illustrator. They have a daughter named Genevieve. Two dogs (whippets), numerous chipmunks, and a visiting mother raccoon make up the rest of the household. Mills was born on December 4, 1957. She recommends writing to her through the publisher Little, Brown & Company, Time Warner Inc., 1271 Avenue of the Americas, New York, NY 10020.

Discussion Questions

Make sixteen photocopies of the rag coat graphic (Figure 12.1). Reproduce the questions (page 168) on white copy paper. Cut and glue them to the back of the rag coats. Laminate, if possible, and cut along the outlines of the coats.

Pass the discussion questions around in a small sewing basket. The rag coats should be face up with the questions hidden from view. Have one child select a rag coat from the basket, read the question aloud, and give his or her opinion or answer. If desired, the discussion can be opened to the group for others to give their viewpoints or thoughts. Then the child passes the basket to the next individual who repeats the process. Allow only one rag coat to be drawn at a time. This prevents others from reading and concentrating on their questions and not listening to what is being discussed.

Remember, some of the discussion questions have more than one answer, or there is no "right" answer. Children may voice a completely different response than expected.

Activities

Quilt Squares Secret Message Activity Sheet

Photocopy the activity sheet (Figure 12.2, page 169) for each child in the book club.

Quilt Squares Secret Message Answer Key

The secret message is: BE KIND TO ONE ANOTHER.

Figure 12.1. Rag Coat for Discussion Questions

Discussion Questions

Have you ever been teased? How did it make you feel?	Have you ever teased someone? Why? How do you feel about it now?
Why did the Quilting Mothers want to make Minna a coat?	Why did Minna hate the dark-colored clothes worn by visitors who came after her father died?
What do you think is meant by the saying "A stitch in time saves nine"?	Why do people wear black to a funeral?
Which is your favorite illustration in the book?	Look at the illustration of Minna and her mother in front of the fireplace. What old-fashioned things can you identify?
How would the story be different if Minna had not returned to talk about the coat?	If you could rewrite the story, what would you change?
What is a keepsake? Do you have a keepsake? Did Minna?	What is the most important thing to own if you want to have a friend?
During the time period of *The Rag Coat* story, there were no televisions, videos, or shopping malls. What did children play or do for fun?	Minna ran into the woods and sat on a log when she was angry. Do you have a place you go when you are mad? What do you do while there?
Have you ever been brave?	Papa said, "People only need people." Do you agree or disagree? Why?

Quilt Squares Secret Message

Starting with A, assign a number below each of the 26 letters of the alphabet. Begin numbering at 1, then proceed in numerical order to 26. Fill in the blanks on the fabric pieces to see the lesson that Minna and her schoolmates learned.

Figure 12.2. Quilt Squares Secret Message Activity Sheet

Hide the Thimble Game

Before television, videos, or computers, children had to be inventive when thinking of things to do if it was too dark or cold to play outside. Guessing games, Drop the Clothespin in the Bottle, or making craft items might have been some of their indoor activities. Some may have knitted, embroidered, or crocheted. If the adult in the family was not using the thimble, it could easily become part of a simple game.

A thimble is a small metal cup worn over a finger to help push the needle through fabric when sewing. Because of its size it can be readily hidden, and allows for a good hide-and-seek activity. Supplies are simple: one thimble. The first chosen to hide the thimble does so while the others hide their eyes and count to twenty-five. The first person to find the thimble becomes the next one to hide it.

Craft

Pretty Paper Rag Coat Craft

✓ **SUPPLIES**

Discarded wallpaper sample books

Glue or glue sticks

8½-by-11-inch construction paper (various colors)

White copy paper

Pinking shears, scissors, or paper cutter

Collect wallpaper sample books from decorating stores. Sample books are regularly discarded because of new, incoming catalogs, so it is easy to gather up several with a few telephone calls.

Tear out pages that have small prints or designs. Large flowers, scenes, or heavy fabric pages are not appropriate. Cut strips into 1-by-1-inch squares. Cut some of these squares into triangles for a variety in the pattern.

Photocopy one rag coat pattern (Figure 12.3) on white paper for each student. Supply each child with glue, scissors, and a number of wallpaper pieces. The children will glue their wallpaper "fabric" pieces onto the pattern and then trim around the outside edge of the rag coat pattern. If possible, provide an assortment of construction paper colors and allow the children to choose their favorite. When finished, they will glue their rag coats onto an 8½-by-11-inch piece of construction paper.

Figure 12.3. Pretty Paper Rag Coat Pattern

Snacks

The following are examples of foods that Minna would have enjoyed at home with her family. Serve one or more of the following items.

Biscuits or cornbread served with jam or honey

Popcorn balls

Gingerbread cookies

Sugar cookies

Juice, milk, or water served in pint or half-pint glass canning jars

---

Other Titles to Share

Birdseye, Tom. *Soap! Soap! Soap! Don't Forget the Soap!: An Appalachian Folktale*. Illustrated by Andrew Glass. New York: Holiday House, 1993. [30 pages]

An amusing tale about a very forgetful boy whose mother sends him to the store for soap and the unfortunate events that take place on that journey.

Coerr, Eleanor. *The Josefina Story Quilt*. Illustrated by Bruce Degen. New York: Harper & Row, 1986. [64 pages]

A young girl works on a quilt as her family travels west in a covered wagon. Her pet hen is an integral part of the adventure.

Ernst, Lisa Campbell. *Sam Johnson and the Blue Ribbon Quilt*. New York: Lothrop, Lee & Shepard, 1983. [32 pages]

Farmer Johnson starts his own quilting club when the women's quilting group scorns the idea of men sewing as well as they can.

Estes, Eleanor. *The Hundred Dresses*. Illustrated by Louis Slobodkin. New York: Harcourt, Brace & World, 1944. [80 pages]

Cruel teasing ensues when a girl wears the same faded dress to school every day, yet tells everyone that she has 100 dresses at home in her closet.

Flournoy, Valerie. *The Patchwork Quilt*. Illustrated by Jerry Pinkney. New York: Dial Books for Young Readers, 1985. [28 pages]

A family is involved in the making of a quilt. The grandmother and young granddaughter become closer in the process.

Franco, Betsy. *Grandpa's Quilt*. Illustrated by Linda A. Bild. New York: Children's Press, 1999. [32 pages]

A beginning reader that is based on a Finnish nonsense story. Anna, Ben, and Lily try to make a short quilt longer so that it will cover Grandpa's cold toes.

Harris, Emmy Lou. "Coat of Many Colors." *Pieces of the Sky*. Warner Brothers, 1990. Compact disc.

Contains the song written by Dolly Parton titled, "Coat of Many Colors."

Hopkinson, Deborah. *Sweet Clara and the Freedom Quilt*. Illustrated by James Ransome. New York: Alfred A. Knopf, 1993. [35 pages]

A young slave girl learns to sew and then helps others to create a quilt with a secret map pattern. The quilt helps her to find the route back to her mother and then North to freedom in Canada.

Houston, Gloria. *My Great-Aunt Arizona*. Illustrated by Susan Condie Lamb. New York: HarperCollins, 1992. [30 pages]

The author tells the story of her aunt who grew up in the Blue Ridge Mountains and becomes an inspiring teacher to many generations of Appalachian children.

Johnston, Tony. *The Quilt Story*. Illustrated by Tomie dePaola. New York: G. P. Putnam's Sons, 1985. [30 pages]

A simple story about a quilt and the families that are a part of its history.

Kinsey-Warnock, Natalie. *The Canada Geese Quilt*. Illustrated by Leslie W. Bowman. New York: E. P. Dutton, 1989. [60 pages]

Ten-year-old Ariel works with her grandmother to create a special quilt for the family's new baby while she deals with issues of birth and death.

Parton, Dolly. *Coat of Many Colors*. Illustrated by Judith Sutton. New York: HarperCollins, 1994. [32 pages]

Lyrics from the country music song of the same title become the text portraying a girl who is teased by other children because the coat her mother sewed for her is made of rags.

———. "Coat of Many Colors." *Coat of Many Colors*. BMG/Buddah Records, 1999. Compact disc.

Dolly Parton's song and book make a good companion to Mills's *The Rag Coat*.

Polocco, Patricia. *The Keeping Quilt*. New York: Simon & Schuster, 1988. [31 pages]

Author's autobiographical story of a family quilt passed from mother to daughter over a century's time.

Rylant, Cynthia. *Appalachia: The Voices of Sleeping Birds*. Illustrated by Barry Moser. San Diego: Harcourt Brace Jovanovich, 1991. [31 pages]

Both Appalachia born, author and illustrator present an honest and beautiful creation about the region and its people. An award-winning title.

Wells, Rosemary. *Mary on Horseback: Three Mountain Stories*. Illustrated by Peter McCarty. New York: Dial Books for Young Readers, 1988. [55 pages]

In 1923, Mary Breckinridge, an affluent young woman, came to the Appalachian Mountains of Kentucky to begin a lifetime of caring for people in the area. The Frontier Nursing Service was formed to honor her devotion and celebrated seventy-five years of service in 2000.

Contacting the Publisher

Contact the marketing department of Little, Brown and Company at Time Warner Inc., 1271 Avenue of the Americas, New York, NY 10020, 212-522-8700, publicity@littlebrown.com, http://www.twbookmark.com. Ask what promotional items they have for *The Rag Coat* such as posters, bookmarks, and the author/illustrator's biography. Request enough for supplies for each child in your book club and your files.

CHAPTER 13

Rattlesnake Dance: True Tales, Mysteries, and Rattlesnake Ceremonies

By Jennifer Owings Dewey

Dewey, Jennifer Owings. *Rattlesnake Dance: True Tales, Mysteries, and Rattlesnake Ceremonies*. Honesdale, PA: Boyds Mills Press, 1997. [48 pages]

Dewey weaves her story of being bit at nine years of age by a prairie rattlesnake, and later attending a Hopi snake dance ceremony, with factual information about rattlers.

Introduction

S nakes fascinate children and adults alike. Their sharp fangs and venom repel us, but their features and habits captivate us. Flicking tongues, narrow eye slits, and wriggling bodies cause one to either move in for a closer look or pull back in fear. The buzz of a rattler's tail is cause for all of us to flee.

Jennifer Dewey was nine years old when she was bit by a prairie rattlesnake. The doctor and her family did not know if she would survive. The clinic in rural New Mexico had no antivenin available. Throughout her ordeal, readers learn the fascinating natural history of rattlesnakes. For example, the venom of a rattlesnake is similar to human saliva. A rattlesnake could suffer an allergic reaction from a human's bite just as a human reacts badly to a rattlesnake's bite.

Amazingly, humans can drink rattlesnake venom with no consequences; it must be injected into the bloodstream to pose any danger.

As the children arrive, serve snacks and hand out the Interhissting Snakey Facts activity sheet (Figure 13.4). Present information about the author/illustrator once everyone has gathered and proceed with the discussion questions. End with the Desert Bingo Game on page 180 or the Rattlesnake Mask craft (Figures 13.5A–D, see pages 189–90).

As an alternative to the Desert Bingo Game, invite a wildlife biologist or naturalist to speak. This individual could be from your state's wildlife conservation department or area zoo. Find a naturalist or biologist who specializes in nongame species, such as birds and reptiles, and who will bring a live (nonvenomous) snake to share.

Introducing the Author/Illustrator

Jennifer Owings Dewey

Used by permission of Jennifer Owings Dewey.

Dewey is a prolific author and illustrator with nearly fifty books (at this writing) to her credit. Most of the books she writes or illustrates are nonfiction titles. She has written two autobiographical stories, *Cowgirl Dreams* (Boyds Mills Press, 1995) and *Navajo Summer* (Boyds Mills Press, 1998), which tell of her childhood growing up on a ranch in New Mexico, north of Santa Fe.

As a child, Dewey says drawing was the one thing she felt she could do well. She had gallery shows, but felt a calling to do something different with her artwork. At thirty years of age she began writing and illustrating books for her own children. She took a trip to New York and showed her artwork to an editor. The editor told Dewey she should also write. This gave Dewey the confidence to write her first book *Clem: The Story of a Raven* (Penguin Putnam, 1986).

Dewey has always been interested in natural history for children. In conducting research for *Rattlesnake Dance*, she spent six months in the deserts of southern Arizona with Harry Greene, curator of reptiles, University of California, Berkeley. Greene and his graduate students work from early spring to early fall studying blacktail rattlesnakes. Snakes are the most active at these seasons.

A prairie rattlesnake had bitten Dewey when she was nine years old. Greene tested Dewey's willingness to ever touch a snake again.

"He placed a female rattlesnake, who was so full she was asleep, in my arms," says Dewey. "The lump in her tummy was a bunny. When they are full like that they have no more venom and no energy."

After six months of research, the writing came fast and furious. Dewey wrote *Rattlesnake Dance* in three weeks and spent another ten weeks illustrating. She worked from the many photographs she had taken and sketches she drew in the field.

Rattlesnake Dance also describes a Hopi snake ceremony that Dewey witnessed with her father. Dewey says it did not terrify her to see the ceremony after her brush with death.

"I grew up being told that you don't survive a rattlesnake bite," says Dewey. "I thought maybe I was a strange kid. When I attended the Hopi snake ceremony (and saw a rattlesnake bite one of the dancers), I wanted to know why . . . how? It was something I wanted to understand, but I never did."

Dewey is a full-time author living in Santa Fe, New Mexico. She may be reached at 607 Old Taos Highway, Santa Fe, NM, 87501.

Discussion Questions

Make sixteen photocopies of the rattlesnake graphic (Figure 13.1, page 178) on tan paper. Reproduce the questions (page 179) on white copy paper. Cut and glue them to the back of the graphics. Laminate, if possible, and cut along the outlines of the rattlesnakes.

Pass the discussion questions around in a drawstring cloth bag. Herpetologists often place snakes they have caught into cloth bags that close with a drawstring. Children will have a lot of fun reaching into the bag to withdraw a rattlesnake graphic. Have one child select a snake from the bag, read the question aloud, and give his or her opinion or answer. If desired, the discussion can be opened to the group for others to give their viewpoints or thoughts. Then the child passes the bag to the next individual who repeats the process. Allow only one rattlesnake to be drawn at a time. This prevents others from reading and concentrating on their questions and not listening to what is being discussed.

Remember, some of the discussion questions have more than one answer, or there is no "right" answer. Children may voice a completely different response than expected.

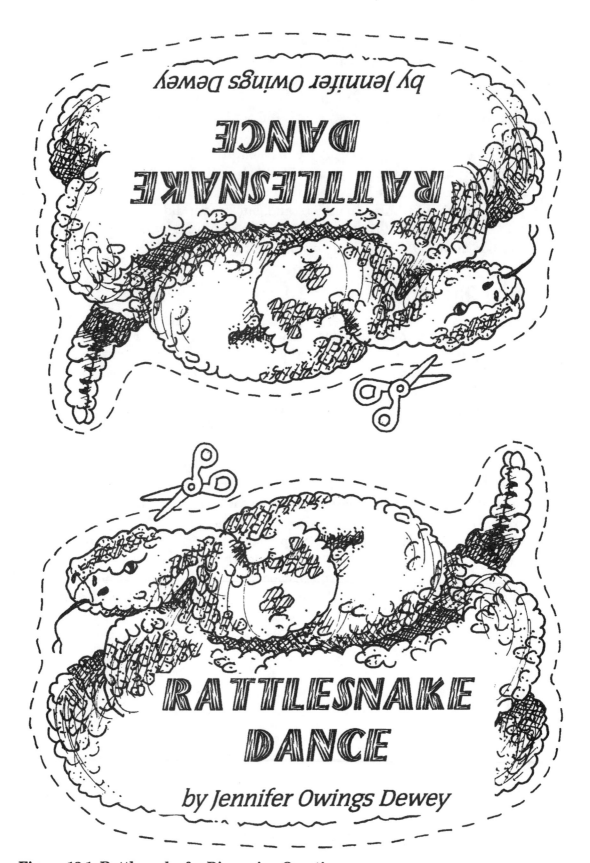

Figure 13.1. Rattlesnake for Discussion Questions

Discussion Questions

Which rattlesnakes have you seen in the wild or at the zoo?	How was the author bit by a rattlesnake?
Why are rattlesnakes called pit vipers?	Why are rattlesnakes different colors?
What happened to the author after she was bit?	Where are rattlesnakes found?
Describe how the Hopi dancers were dressed.	Which state has the biggest rattlesnakes?
Does a baby rattlesnake have a full rattle at the end of its tail?	How is a rattlesnake able to swallow a whole mouse?
Which part of the book is your favorite?	Describe your favorite illustration.
What is an interesting fact about rattlesnakes?	How do rattlesnakes fight?
Do rattlesnakes have big brains or small brains?	Have you ever touched a snake? If so, what did it feel like?

Activities

Desert Bingo Game

Figure 13.2. Desert Bingo Board Sketch

✓ **SUPPLIES**

8½-by-11-inch white copy paper

Lightweight poster board (a 10-by-10-inch piece for each child)

Game pieces (coins, 1-inch circles or squares, small crackers, and so forth)

Bingo squares for the game board (Figures 13.3A–T)

Scissors or paper cutter (adult use only)

Colored pencils (optional)

Directions

Use the twenty bingo squares (Figures 13.3A–T, pages 181–84) to create a unique game board for each player. Photocopy one set of the bingo squares for each child. Using a paper cutter or scissors, cut out each of the squares. Select sixteen of the twenty bingo squares to make one game board. Place four squares across and four squares down on a photocopier and copy. To make each game board unique, choose different squares and arrange in different combinations.

Glue each game board to a 10-by-10-inch piece of lightweight poster board. Laminate the entire board to create a smooth playing surface. (Optional: Color the bingo squares with colored pencils before laminating.)

To make the game pieces, cut out 1-inch circles or squares or use other items, such as pennies, plastic game pieces pirated from other games, small crackers, or pieces of cereal.

How the Game Is Played

The game leader has a laminated set of all twenty bingo squares (cut out but not glued to a game board). He draws out the pieces one by one from a container. As the game pieces are drawn, he calls out what he has selected, for example, "scorpion," "tortoise," "rattlesnake," and so forth. The children find the matching picture on their game boards and place a game piece over the picture. The first child to cover four pictures in a row with game pieces calls out "bingo!" and is the winner. (An alternative method is for the first child to have all pictures covered to call out "bingo.")

The game leader should move at a steady pace and not go back to repeat a picture. This game helps children scan the board quickly for matching patterns.

A. Saguaro Cactus

B. Kangaroo Rat

C. Tortoise

D. Cactus Flower

E. Rattlesnake

F. Coyote

Figure 13.3. Desert Bingo Squares

G. Zebra-Tailed Lizard

H. Jackrabbit

I. Tarantula

J. Conenose Bug

K. Scorpion

L. Bighorn Sheep

Figure 13.3. Desert Bingo Squares

M. Elf Owl

N. Roadrunner

O. Peccary

P. Prickly Pear Cactus

Q. Bobcat

R. Toad

Figure 13.3. Desert Bingo Squares

S. Mule Deer

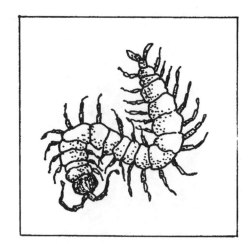

T. Centipede

Figure 13.3. Desert Bingo Squares

Interhissting Snakey Facts Activity Sheet

Photocopy the activity sheet (Figure 13.4, page 186) for each child in the book club.

Snake-Loving Guest Speaker

Invite a naturalist or biologist from your state's wildlife conservation department to speak to your book club. Check the government section of your phone book to locate the telephone number. To ensure that your speaker will be interesting to children, ask for an individual who has experience with school or library visits.

Many state wildlife conservation departments have individuals who visit schools and libraries as part of their outreach efforts. These individuals will come at no charge. A good speaker will have a slide or video presentation, and/or hands-on items to share, such as a live (nonvenomous) snake, snake skeleton, snake skin, and so forth. Other places to contact a speaker may be a natural history museum or zoo.

When making arrangements with the speaker, confirm the date of the presentation, what time the speaker should arrive, how long the speaker is expected to speak, and what information will be covered. Ask what equipment is needed, such as a slide projector and screen or television and VCR. Will the speaker need a table for hands-on items? Confirm that the presentation is free or confirm the price for the presentation.

Make certain that the speaker has the address of where the program will take place and a telephone number to call in case a problem arises. Ask the speaker for a mailing address and tell the speaker you will send a letter of confirmation. See sample letter of confirmation on page 187.

A week before the scheduled presentation, call the speaker and again confirm the date, time, and location. Have a backup activity in case an emergency or illness prevents your speaker from visiting that day.

After the presentation, be sure to write a thank-you note, or send thank-you notes written by the children. Speakers appreciate this meaningful gesture of appreciation.

Note for school media specialist or teachers: If you call a speaker that is some distance away, arrange for him or her to spend a couple of hours at the school. The speaker can speak to several classrooms or make a couple of presentations in the media center. Arrange for lunch before your speaker returns to his or her office.

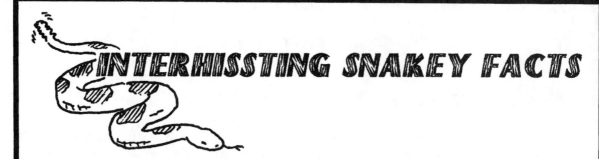

List as many different facts about rattlesnakes that you can remember. Work with a friend and see how many you can list together. At the bottom of the page, draw a picture of a rattlesnake.

1.

2.

3.

4.

5.

6.

Figure 13.4. Interhissting Snakey Facts Activity Sheet

SAMPLE LETTER OF CONFIRMATION

Date

Briarwood School
1000 Snowball Lane
Maple Leaf, State 00000

Melinda Hickman
State Department of Wildlife Conservation
1801 N. Washington Avenue
Maple Leaf, State 00001

Dear Ms. Hickman:

Thank you for agreeing to visit Briarwood School on Thursday, January 20, 2001, from 12:45–1:30 p.m. As discussed in our telephone conversation, Briarwood's book club will be ready to hear your thirty-minute presentation about snakes in our state. The book club is a reading group of sixteen students who are in the first through third grades.

For your presentation, I will have a television and VCR plus a table for hands-on items. Call me if there is something else that you need.

The address of the school is listed above. I have enclosed a map with driving directions for your convenience. When you arrive please park in front and come to the office, which is right inside the front door. The secretary will call me, and I will come to meet you. If you encounter any problems, the telephone number at school is 000-691-4555.

We are looking forward to your presentation.

Sincerely,

Jeanne Bugg
School Media Specialist

Craft

Rattlesnake Mask Craft

✓ **SUPPLIES**

Construction paper (various colors including red, white, and black)

Lightweight poster board

Pencils

Scissors

Crayons

Glue

Single-hole punch

Adhesive tape

Yarn

To prepare this craft for the children, use Figures 13.5A–D to trace and cut out several rattlesnake mask pattern pieces from lightweight poster board. On the day of the book club meeting, provide children with the supplies listed above plus the poster board templates (Figures 13.5A–D).

Using the pattern pieces and pencils, each child will trace and cut out the following items from construction paper:

- One mask (any color is fine except white, black, and red)

- Two fangs (white construction paper)

- Two heat-sensing pits (black construction paper)

- One tongue (red construction paper)

To create a rattlesnake mask, cut out the holes for the eyes and nose. Glue the heat-sensing pits, fangs, and tongue into place. The heat-sensing pits are located near the nose. For a description and illustration, see page 11 of *Rattlesnake Dance*.

Punch a hole on each side of the mask using a single-hole punch and tie an 18-inch piece of yarn to each hole. Children will use the yarn to tie the mask around their heads. To prevent the yarn from cutting through the construction paper, place a double layer of adhesive tape over the areas before punching holes.

A. Mask

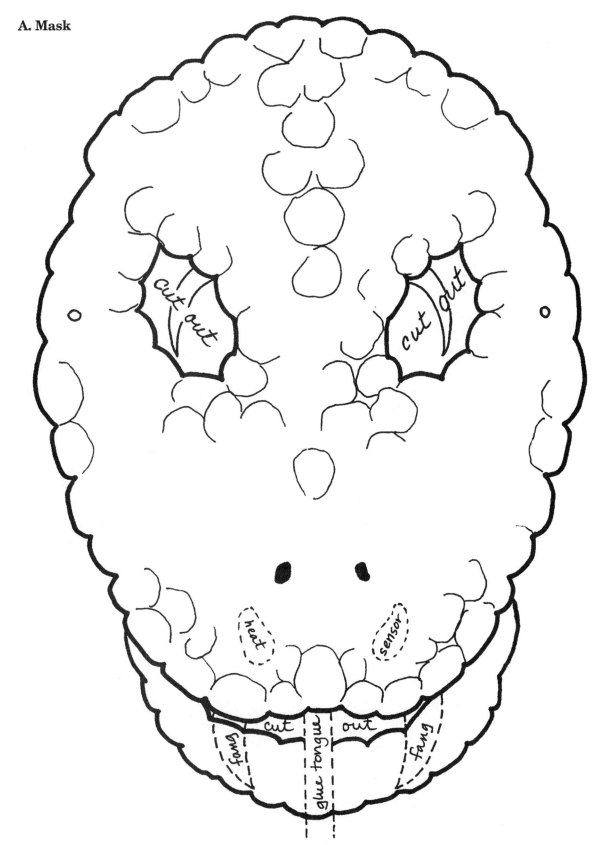

Figure 13.5. Rattlesnake Mask Patterns

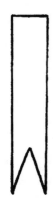

B. Tongue
(Cut out one of red construction paper)

C. Heat-Sensing Pit
(Cut out two of black construction paper)

D. Fang
(Cut out two of white construction paper)

Figure 13.5. Rattlesnake Mask Patterns

Snacks

Serve something "snakey" for the children to enjoy. Choose one of the following suggestions:

Create snakes using soft bread sticks, red string licorice, and raisins. Use a toothpick to make a hole at the end of the breadstick. Insert a 2-inch piece of red string licorice. Open two additional holes at the top, near the mouth. Press raisins into the holes to create two eyes. Make one snake per child. Serve with string cheese.

Pancakes are always a favorite. Pour the batter into an electric skillet creating long, thin, curvy snakes. Serve with butter and syrup or jam.

Serve veggies that are cut long and thin, such as carrots, celery, and cucumbers. Serve with ranch dressing, sour cream dip, or peanut butter.

Spread cream cheese on a soft, flour tortillas; roll and slice. Tell the kids they are coiled snakes.

Other Titles to Share

Arnosky, Jim. *All About Rattlesnakes*. New York: Scholastic Press, 1997. [26 pages]

The illustrations by Arnosky make this title unique. They explain concepts photographs cannot, such as how the segments of the rattle interlock or how the belly scales move the snake along.

Ata, Te. Adapted by Lynn Moroney. *Baby Rattlesnake*. Illustrated by Veg Reisberg. San Francisco: Children's Book Press, 1989. [32 pages]

In this Chickasaw Indian legend, Baby Rattlesnake pesters the Rattlesnake People until he gets his rattle—something he is not ready for.

Burns, Diane L. *Snakes Alive!: Jokes About Snakes*. Illustrated by Joan Hanson. Minneapolis: Lerner Publications, 1988. [34 pages]

This is a selection of easy-to-read jokes about snakes that are "hiss-terically" amusing.

Czernecki, Stefan, and Timothy Rhodes. *The Singing Snake*. Illustrated by Stefan Czernecki. New York: Hyperion Books for Children, 1993. [40 pages]

Snake swallows Lark to win a singing contest but only ends up with a "hiss" in this Australian folktale.

Gray, Libba Moore. *Small Green Snake*. Illustrated by Holly Meade. New York: Orchard Books, 1994. [32 pages]

Sassy, flashy, Small Green Snake finds adventure in his garden. The word play makes for a great read aloud, and the torn-paper artwork inspires art projects for the classroom.

Johnson, Angela. *The Girl Who Wore Snakes*. Illustrated by James E. Ransome. New York: Orchard Books, 1993. [32 pages]

Ali discovers a love for snakes that not all friends and family members share.

Markle, Sandra. *Outside and Inside Snakes*. New York: Macmillan Books for Young Readers, 1995. [40 pages]

A factual book about snakes in general. Outstanding photography, by different photographers, shows such topics as a snake's internal organs and venom at the end of a fang.

McDonald, Mary Ann. *Rattlesnakes*. Illustrated by Joe McDonald. Minneapolis: Capstone Press, 1996. [48 pages]

A well-done factual book about rattlesnakes that is nicely illustrated with color photographs. Includes a lot of close-ups of many types of rattlesnakes.

Nygaard, Elizabeth. *Snake Alley Band*. Illustrated by Betsy Lewin. New York: Bantam, Doubleday Dell, 1998. [32 pages]

A small snake discovers the musical sounds of other animals in Snake Alley, Lake Minneoko.

Olaleye, Isaac. *Lake of the Big Snake: An African Rain Forest Adventure*. Illustrated by Claudia Shepard. Honesdale, PA: Boyds Mills Press, 1998. [32 pages]

Two boys, Ade and Tayo, must outwit a large water snake to return home safely.

Slotboom, Wendy. *King Snake*. Illustrated by John Manders. Boston: Houghton Mifflin, 1997. [32 pages]

Henry and Tinkerton, two mice, use their wits to escape a talkative garter snake named King Snake.

Smith, Mavis. *A Snake Mistake*. New York: Penguin Putnam, 1998. [32 pages]

Jake, the snake, swallows two lightbulbs when raiding the chicken coop. Based on a true story, this is a Puffin Science Easy-to-Read title.

Watkins, Sherrin. *Green Snake Ceremony*. Illustrated by Kim Doner. Tulsa, OK: Council Oak Books, 1995. [36 pages]

Mary (Wpapiyeshi) Greyfeather helps her grandfather find a snake for her green snake ceremony. Illustrations of a green snake, living under the house, tell a humorous second story.

Contacting the Publisher

Contact the marketing department at Boyds Mills Press, 815 Church Street, Honesdale, PA 18431, 800-490-5111 or 570-253-1164; http://www.boydsmillspress .com. Ask what promotional items they have for *Rattlesnake Dance: True Tales, Mysteries, and Rattlesnake Ceremonies* such as posters, bookmarks, and the author/illustrator's biography. Request enough supplies for each child in your book club and your files.

CHAPTER 14

Some Frog!

By Eve Bunting

Illustrated by Scott Medlock

Bunting, Eve. *Some Frog!* Illustrated by Scott Medlock. San Diego: Harcourt Brace, 1998. [45 pages]

> *Young Billy looks forward to his father coming to help him catch a frog for the frog-jumping competition at his school. When the father does not arrive as promised, Billy's mother and grandparents help make the day's events a family success.*

Introduction

Frogs and toads have been in existence for millions of years and scientists have identified over 3,000 different species. Many sizes of frogs exist, from the tiny Spring Peeper, which is no larger than a half-inch long, to the really large Goliath Frog that lives in southern Africa. The latter grows to be as big as a small dog, weighing as much as three pounds.

What is the difference between frogs and toads? There are two distinct characteristics. Frogs are always wet and slimy to the touch, and they hop. Toads do not hop, they walk, and toads are always dry and have rough skin.

Before the session begins, prepare for the children to play the Frog Life Cycle Game. Place the Frog Life Cycle icons (Figure 14.4) in a small bucket, like the one Billy used to catch Amphibian. As the children arrive, ask them to select one of the Frog Life Cycle icons from the bucket. After they have seen what icon they have selected, tape the image to the child's forehead and direct them to sit with others wearing the same symbol. See more details about this game on page 200.

Begin the program by serving some of the suggested froggy snacks. They are sure to garner appreciative exclamations of "ooooooh, gross!" and "yuck," along with lots of smiles and giggles when it is announced what the food items are meant to depict. Green punch as swamp water and green olives as frog's eyes are two examples. Distribute the Some Frog! Hidden Message Activity Sheet (Figure 14.3) and pencils for a warm-up exercise.

Share some of the information about frogs from the introductory paragraphs and then proceed with the author and illustrator biographies. Play the Frog Life Cycle Game and then move into the discussion of the story.

Give a Some Reader! Medal (Figure 14.2) to everyone after the discussion ends to emphasize that the interaction and sharing of ideas makes everyone a winner. If time allows, distribute craft supplies for the Origami Frog Craft (Figure 14.5) and end with a frog-jumping contest as explained on page 204. Otherwise, make photocopies of the origami frog instructions available for the students to take home.

Introducing the Author and Illustrator

Eve Bunting

Photo by Hans Gutknecht. Courtesy of Harcourt Inc.

Early in 1999, Eve Bunting's family and friends attended a party in her honor. The thrill of the evening occurred when Mrs. Bunting's two sons made a surprise entrance into the restaurant, each holding 100 balloons. It was not Bunting's 200th birthday, nor did she win a contest for eating 200 eggrolls. The balloons represented the 200th book that Eve Bunting had just published. And, amazingly, she is not out of ideas yet. This prolific writer states, "Everyday I get ideas for what might be another good book!"

Bunting writes mostly picture books and some short chapter books. *The Summer of Riley* (Harper-Collins, 2001), about a boy who adopts an animal shelter dog, is her first book for middle school readers.

A brand new genre for Bunting these days is nonfiction. She recounts, "In a book for Troll Book Club called *Dreaming of America*, I wrote a fictionalized account of an Irish girl named Annie Moore, who was the first immigrant to step foot on Ellis Island. It's an imagined journey that I created after many, many hours of research about America in the late 1800s."

Many readers may not realize what a great deal of research must be completed even for a short picture book with a simple story line.

"When working on the Annie Moore book (*Dreaming of America: An Ellis Island Story*, Bridge Water Books, 2000), I had a lot of communication with the Ellis Island Library. The librarian (Barry Moreno) and I became good friends. He told me about some of the many family gatherings that were held on the island, and from those conversations, a picture book called *A Picnic in October* (Harcourt Brace, 1999) was created.

"On that same note, when I wrote *So Far from the Sea* (Clarion Books, 1998), a story about a family who makes a return visit to their Japanese internment camp, I did an extensive amount of research about the conditions surrounding World War II and America's state of mind during those troubling times. I certainly never want to misrepresent historical information in any book that I do."

The author was born in Maghera, Ireland, on December 18, 1928. The house in which she was born had been the house of her father and grandfather, as well. Storytelling was a nightly "after lights out" activity at Eve's boarding school and, when at home on holidays, reading was a favorite pastime for the entire family.

"I have such fond memories of sitting in my father's lap while he read books like *Treasure Island*, *The Swiss Family Robinson*, and *Kidnapped* to me. My father loved poetry and he often read poetry aloud to me."

When Bunting was older, and read on her own, the Anne of Green Gables series was her favored choice, and she remembers pretending that she was the character Anne. Bunting never lost her love for those books. A few years ago, she fulfilled a lifelong dream by traveling to Prince Edward Island, the setting for the L. M. Montgomery stories.

"My mother, a reader like my dad, taught me about the importance of books, reading, and literature," shares the author. "She began a library in our hometown in County Derry, Ireland. And, although, she loved to see me lost in a book on a rainy day, and it did rain a lot in Ireland, she invariably would send me outside for some fresh air whenever the rain stopped."

Today Bunting lives in sunny southern California with her husband of fifty years. (Mr. Bunting loves books too.) The couple has lived in the same house since 1961, and it is there that Bunting writes almost every day. She writes about a great variety of subjects and themes, such as the Vietnam Veterans Memorial Wall, the Los Angeles city riots, holidays, the importance of trees, and the Orphan Trains. Bunting has three grown children and four granddaughters.

Bunting likes to create action stories with an underlying message. For *Some Frog!*, the message is an important one. The author believes that, "sometimes you might have to settle for something less, but you still appreciate what you have.

"My favorite part of *Some Frog!* is when Billy asks his mom to go to the baseball game. I especially love the illustrations that Scott Medlock did for my story."

Eve Bunting welcomes correspondence through Harcourt Inc., 525 B Street, Suite 1900, San Diego, CA 92101.

Scott Medlock

Photo by Howard Kaplan. Courtesy of Harcourt Inc.

Scott Medlock was a very busy child, and he is still a very busy man. Always a high achiever, Medlock not only earned straight A's as a student ("I was very into school") but competed in football, baseball, and track and field. He also participated in the martial arts and was a boxer.

One might surmise that young Medlock read *Sports Illustrated* or biographies about famous athletes. Actually, he enjoyed books about American artist N. C. Wyeth, and relished looking at the art that Wyeth produced. A sign of the future? Yes, it was, because today he is a successful artist who combines his love of sports with his passion for drawing and painting.

Medlock's works have been exhibited worldwide, from Los Angeles to New York to Tokyo. He has won many awards for his wide range of accomplishments in fine arts and illustration. He produces lithographs, posters, children's books, book jackets, and advertising. Commissioned works include portraits of Presidents Ronald Reagan and George Bush Sr., as well as many actors, entertainers, and sports figures. Some of his corporate clients include Pepsi and AT&T, and corporate offices around the world display his vibrant oil paintings.

His works are also on display at http://www.scottmedlock.com. In the next few years there are plans for Scott Medlock galleries. "I am very excited about the development of my galleries. It will make for great family trips when we travel," Medlock explains.

Other aspects of Medlock's life keep him busy. He has a wife named Myrna and two young sons. "We live in southern California in a house that has a manmade cascading waterfall in the backyard. This is where I like to go for inspiration. In the evenings I enjoy listening to the frogs croaking."

Medlock graduated from the prestigious Art Center College of Design in Pasadena. Many renowned artists and illustrators are alumni of the college. "I had not thought about illustrating children's books after I finished college; however, when Diane D'Andrade, senior editor at Harcourt Inc., called me about illustrating Lee Bennett Hopkins's book called *Extra Innings: Baseball Poems* (see "Other Titles to Share" in this chapter), I agreed to the project. Each poem in the book called for a different illustration. I liked the idea of my art being a stimulating part of the whole."

Extra Innings received many honors including the 1994 Southern California Council on Literature for Children and Young People's Excellence in Illustration award. Hopkins and Medlock worked together on another book in 1996 called *Opening Days: Sport Poems* (see "Other Titles to Share").

"When Diane D'Andrade sent the *Some Frog!* manuscript for me to read, I did not expect to feel the emotions that I did. I had such an immediate flood of mental images of how I wanted to illustrate the story. I was very much involved with the story line from the very first reading of it."

Medlock's nephew modeled as Billy. The two drove to a nearby stream to capture a frog—to realistically live the experience. "That frog was my nephew's pet for quite a while. He even made the frog mask that is illustrated in the book.

"My sister modeled for Billy's mom and my dad became the grandfather of the story," says the artist. "When my nephew posed for the picture where Billy is at the window waiting for his dad, sincere emotions were being evoked because of situations going on in his young life at the time. I couldn't wait to get to my studio and paint the feelings that I had observed and sketched. Emotional qualities are a big part of all my work. I don't want to be so technical in my craft that my art becomes lifeless."

Medlock especially enjoys book signings when young readers are present, and he loves the great questions that children ask.

"Children are so pointed about their opinions. They don't hesitate to let me know where they think I fell short in my illustrations, or perhaps what they feel I may have left out! I love their honesty. The interaction with them will only make me a much more mature illustrator."

Medlock welcomes correspondence through Harcourt Inc., 525 B Street, Suite 1900, San Diego, CA 92101.

Discussion Questions

Make sixteen photocopies of the frog graphic (Figure 14.1, page 198) on green paper. Reproduce the questions (page 199) on white copy paper. Cut and glue to them the back of the frogs. Laminate, if possible, and cut along the outlines of the frogs.

Pass the discussion questions around in a small bucket. The frogs should be face up with the questions hidden from view. Have one child select a frog from the bucket, read the question aloud, and give his or her opinion or answer. If desired, the discussion can be opened to the group for others to give their viewpoints or thoughts. Then the child passes the bucket to the next individual who repeats the process. Allow only one frog to be drawn at a time. This prevents others from reading and concentrating on their questions and not listening to what is being discussed.

Remember, some of the discussion questions have more than one answer, or there is no "right" answer. Children may voice a completely different response than expected.

Figure 14.1. Frog for Discussion Questions

Discussion Questions

Why do you think frogs croak?	Tell us about Billy's dream.
Give your opinion about the old saying, "It's not whether you win or lose; it's how you play the game."	Amphibian's throat "bulges and wilts" as Billy gets him ready to jump. Show what this might look like.
Which is your favorite illustration? Why?	Which is your favorite part of the story? Why?
Billy thinks the water of Miller's Pond looks "dark as Penzoil." What do you think that means?	Have you ever entered an animal into a pet show or competition? What was it like?
What did Billy's dad teach him?	What did Billy's mom and grandparents teach him?
Tell what you think is the most important thing about being in a contest.	List the three tips that Billy's grandpa gave him about frog-jumping? Which one do you like the best?
As best you can, state the definition of a "family."	If you won a sporting event, which song would you want played as you received your medal?
Have you ever caught a wild creature and let it go again?	In which Olympic event would you like to compete?

Activities

Some Reader! Medal

Photocopy and cut out a Some Reader! medal for each child in the book club (Figure 14.2, page 201).

Some Frog! Hidden Message Activity Sheet

Photocopy the activity sheet (Figure 14.3, page 202) for each child in the book club.

Some Frog! Hidden Message Answer Key

The secret message is: Amphibian was a great jumper!

Frog Life Cycle Game

To introduce the life cycle of the frog, photocopy the pattern sheet (Figure 14.4, page 203) on green paper. Make as many copies as necessary so that each participant will be able to have one of the following six icons: the eggs, the jelly baby, the legless tadpole, the legged tadpole, the froglet, or the adult frog. For example, if there are eighteen children in the group, three copies of the life-cycle pattern sheet will need to be made.

Cut out the individual pictures and place them in a small bucket. Allow each child to draw one and look at it as he arrives. Have small strips of tape ready so that the icon can be stuck to the child's forehead. This will bring about some giggles, but learning comes easily when it is fun. Ask the children to sit with others wearing the same icon.

Direct the young readers to define the order of development, from egg to adult frog. Ask them to stand in line to form the correct order. Assistance from an adult may be necessary to bring about the correct order.

The pattern sheet may also be used as a take-home coloring page.

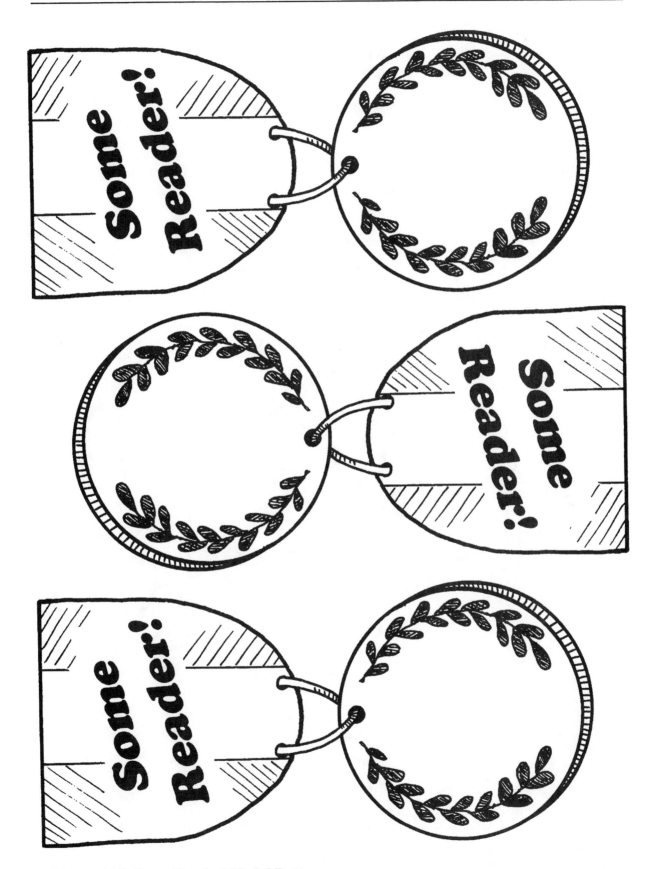

Figure 14.2. Some Reader! Medal Patterns

SOME FROG!
Hidden Message

Find the hidden message on the back of the frog. Hint: Begin at letter A in the lower, right-hand corner.

Figure 14.3. Some Frog! Hidden Message Activity Sheet

Figure 14.4. Frog Life Cycle Game Pattern

Craft

Origami Frog Craft and Jumping Contest

✓ **SUPPLIES**

4-by-6-inch green index cards or green tagboard cut to 4-by-6-inch size (one for each child)

Crayons or markers

Rulers or quarters (one for each child)

Masking tape

Plastic tape measurer or yard stick

Chalk (optional)

Distribute a copy of the origami frog instructions (Figure 14.5, page 205) to each child. Make a frog in front of the group and have everyone follow along.

Use a ruler or coin to help crease the folds. Sharp creases will make for better jumping frogs. Use crayons or markers to make each frog unique. Some children may want to add spots or numbers on their frogs' backs.

This game can be played using a floor or table surface. For a starting line, place a length of masking tape on either the floor or a large rectangular table. To measure the jumps, place a measuring tape or yardstick to one side of the jumping area. Mark the distances with chalk or small pieces of tape and write the children's initials. After some practice hops, allow the young readers to decide if they want to determine the winner from one jump or the longest jump out of three tries.

Origami Frog Craft Directions

Photocopy the craft sheet (Figure 14.5) for each child in the book club.

Origami Frog

Begin with a 4-by-6-inch green index card, or green tagboard cut to a 4-by-6-inch size. As each fold is made (see directions below), use the edge of a ruler or use a coin to help make sharp creases. Sharp creases make for better jumping frogs.

Fold the index card as directed by the illustrations below. Start with the first row, first picture, and go left to right. When finished folding, you may want to decorate your frog's back with spots or a number.

Figure 14.5. Origami Frog Craft Directions

Snacks

Children will enjoy eating as many of these froggy snacks that the adult moderator wants to provide. For drinks, choose either the swamp water or the pond scum.

Swamp water (green punch, limeade, or juice)

Pond scum (pistachio ice cream shakes)

Frog eyes (green or black olives)

Frog eggs on lily pads (green grapes or green gelatin on lettuce)

Toasted frogs (green sugar cookies)

Tadpoles (chocolate drops)

Frog lips (pieces of licorice string)

Other Titles to Share

Amphibian. Eyewitness series. Written by David Hanson. Directed by Peter Miller. 35 min. New York: Dorling Kindersley Vision, 1994. Videocassette.

Presents information and stunning visuals about frogs, toads, and salamanders.

Bunting, Eve. *Once upon a Time*. Photographs by John Pezaris. Katonah, NY: Richard C. Owen, 1995. [32 pages]

Concise, personable autobiography with pleasing photos of the author's family, present as well as past.

Butterworth, Nick, and Mick Inkpen. *Field Day*. New York: Delacorte Press, 1993. [24 pages]

Races and competitions involve children and parents alike at a school event.

Chang, Heidi. *Elaine and the Flying Frog*. New York: Random House, 1988. [62 pages]

Schoolgirls interested in frogs turn their science project into a frog kite.

Clarke, Barry. *Amazing Frogs & Toads*. Eyewitness Junior series. Photographs by Jerry Young. New York: Alfred A. Knopf, 1990. [31 pages]

Exquisite photographs and definitive drawings are combined with an interesting and concise text.

Fleischman, Sid. *McBroom and the Great Race*. Illustrated by Walter Lorraine. Boston: Little, Brown, 1980. [57 pages]

In amusing tall-tale style, Josh McBroom races ornery Heck Jones. The winner gets the amazing McBroom farm.

Hennessey, B. G. *Olympics!* Illustrated by Michael Chesworth. New York: Penguin Books, 1996. [32 pages]

> Jaunty and compelling, this book is a good introduction to the summer and winter Olympic games.

Holmes, Kevin J. *Frogs*. Mankato: MN: Bridgestone Books, 1998. [24 pages]

> Distinctive color photographs illustrate one-page sections that introduce a frog's physical characteristics, habits, life stages, and so forth.

Hopkins, Lee Bennett, ed. *Opening Days: Sports Poems*. Illustrated by Scott Medlock. San Diego: Harcourt Brace, 1996. [37 pages]

> Inspiring, child-oriented poetry illustrated with colorful, action-filled artwork. This is a good read-aloud.

James, Betsy. *Tadpoles*. New York: Dutton, 1999. [30 pages]

> This fictional picture book story is punctuated with science facts. Gives advice on caring for tadpoles. Intriguing cutaway pictures show tadpoles' growth. Afterward provides frog life cycle chart.

Kessler, Leonard. *Old Turtle's Winter Games*. New York: Greenwillow Books, 1983. [48 pages]

> Old Turtle organizes the animals for Olympic-type competitions.

Lewis, Paul Owen. *Frog Girl*. Hillsboro, OR: Beyond Words, 1997. [30 pages]

> Beautiful illustrations by the author support a retelling of a folktale from the native people of the Pacific Northwest Coast about a young girl who aids a mysterious parallel world inhabited by frogs.

The Magic School Bus Hops Home. Based on the series by Joanna Cole and Bruce Degen. 30 min. New York: Scholastic, 1995. Videocassette.

> Miss Frizzle and her classroom learn about the needs of a frog.

Ross, Gayle. *How Turtle's Back Was Cracked: A Traditional Cherokee Tale*. Illustrated by Murv Jacob. New York: Dial, 1995. [32 pages]

> Turtle makes the wolves angry, and in a similar vein to Brer Rabbit, Turtle begs the wolves not to throw him into the river. The results create a lasting impression.

Roth, Susan L. *The Biggest Frog in Australia*. New York: Simon & Schuster, 1996. [33 pages]

> Retelling of an Australian folktale about a thirsty frog that drinks all the world's water. Native animals work to reverse the dire situation. Includes brilliant collage art.

Stefoff, Rebecca. *Frog*. New York: Marshall Cavendish, 1997. [32 pages]

> Numerous, clear photographs and clear text define the physical characteristics and behavior of the frog.

Stevenson, James. *The Mud Flat Olympics*. New York: Greenwillow Books, 1994. [56 pages]

> It is Olympics Day at the mud flat, and all the animals compete with much humor and a great deal of sportsmanship.

Velthuijs, Max. *Frog in Winter*. New York: Tambourine Books, 1992. [26 pages]
Frog finds it difficult to cope when winter comes, so his friends help.

Contacting the Publisher

Contact the marketing department of Harcourt Inc., 525 B Street, Suite 1900, San Diego, CA 92101, 619-699-6716, http://www.harcourtbooks.com. Ask what promotional items they have for *Some Frog!*, such as posters, bookmarks, and the author's and illustrator's biographies. Request enough supplies for each child in your book club and your files.

CHAPTER 15

This Land Is Your Land

By Woody Guthrie
Illustrated by Kathy Jakobsen

Guthrie, Woody. *This Land Is Your Land*. Illustrated by Kathy Jakobsen. Words and music by Woody Guthrie. Boston: Little, Brown, 1998. [36 pages]

> *One of America's best-loved folk songs is illuminated with richly detailed folk art of the country's diverse people and places. Included is a tribute from folksinger Pete Seeger, a biographical scrapbook of Guthrie, and the musical score.*

Introduction

Woody Guthrie has often been called America's most important musician and songwriter of the early twentieth century. He has also been called a folk hero and legend. Much like the traveling minstrels of the Middle Ages, Guthrie wrote songs about events and important issues of the times. Some of his compositions were instruments of social protest, while others, like the children's songs inspired by his own youngsters, were created for the joy of entertainment. Woody Guthrie is credited for writing over 1,000 pieces of music during his lifetime.

Much of Guthrie's work represented his unconventional life experiences. In the late 1920s, after a series of tragedies struck his family, he began roaming the United States on his own as a young teenager. He met and traveled with migrant workers. He befriended destitute families trying to escape the 1930s Dust Bowl region, and spent time with people who were victims of the Great Depression. He hitchhiked, walked, and rode the railroad boxcars back and forth across the Midwest and western United States. He worked at a variety of jobs making very little money, all the while singing for the common people as he played his harmonica and guitar.

Although he had a limited formal education, Woody Guthrie found the world around him intensely interesting. He studied science, economics, religion, and politics throughout his life. The prolific musician was also an author, an artist, a newspaper columnist, a radio-show star, a political activist, and a World War II veteran. Guthrie's music is recorded on many record albums and documented by the Library of Congress.

Numerous musical legends including Bob Dylan, Bruce Springsteen, Leadbelly, Pete Seeger, the group Peter, Paul and Mary, and many more were influenced by Guthrie. Even today his compositions have remained influential as folk song standards.

Woodrow Wilson Guthrie was born in Okemah, Oklahoma in 1912, and died in 1967 of a degenerative nerve disease that had limited his creative output for years. Although he experienced many personal hardships in his life, his songs were often joyful and positive. His musical masterpiece "This Land Is Your Land" describes the beauty of the America he loved. Some have suggested the song would make a worthy national anthem because of the simplicity of both the tune and lyrics.

Set the mood by starting the session with music. Play a recorded version of Woody Guthrie singing "This Land Is Your Land." If possible, seek out the Weston Woods video (see "Other Titles to Share" in this chapter). The video does an exemplary job of showcasing the art of Kathy Jakobsen, along with Woody and his son Arlo singing the song. Nora Guthrie, Woody's daughter, narrates the short biographical presentation. (Nora Guthrie is the executive director of the Woody Guthrie Foundation and Archives in New York City [www.woodyguthrie.org].) Recorded versions of some of Woody's children's songs (see "Other Titles to Share" in this chapter) are also available and make for great listening fun.

For musical interaction, consider distributing inexpensive, plastic kazoos to each of the young readers for a kazoo-along. Even the shyest children, who would not opt to sing aloud, will usually hum along to music when they have kazoos in their mouths. And because the tune to "This Land Is Your Land" is so elegantly simple, the group will be able to create an immediate kazoo concert. You may opt to make available the verses of "This Land Is Your Land" for a group sing-along. The words and music to "This Land Is Your Land" are printed in the back of Jakobsen's book.

Place "snacks for the road" into small, brown paper bags tied closed with macramé cord. These will portray travel knapsacks that Woody Guthrie might have used. Guthrie discovered America by walking, hitchhiking, and traveling in railroad boxcars. You may want to pour the refreshment drinks from a thermos or canteen. While the students are eating, consider distributing The Places I've Been Activity Map (Figure 15.2) for them to color, or the entire group could interact with the This Land Is a Great Land Game on page 215.

Woody Guthrie spent time in hobo camps where campfires were an integral part of food preparation and warmth, plus a gathering place. To illustrate this aspect of the songwriter's life, hold the discussion session around an artificial campfire. Stack logs or sticks in a pile on the floor and place rocks in a ring around the wood. If you wish to simulate a nighttime get-together, place a flashlight under the wood and dim the lights. Of course, a hootenanny around the campfire would be in order once the children are in place. See "Other Titles to Share" in this chapter for song suggestions.

The discussion questions can be passed around in a very small suitcase or duffel bag to emphasize the traveling aspect of the book. If a black cast-iron soup pot or skillet is available, the questions can be placed in the utensil and situated on the campfire logs. Children can reach into the pot or skillet to draw their questions.

Lead into the craft activity America Is Beautiful Travel Sticker (Figure 15.3) with a short explanation of the popularity of suitcase travel labels of times past. If possible, have some to show the group. Children can design a travel sticker for a place they have been or a place they hope to travel to in the future. Be sure to have "This Land Is Your Land" playing softly in the background during the activity.

Introducing the Illustrator

Kathy Jakobsen

Courtesy of Little, Brown and Company, Boston, MA.

Kathy Jakobsen is a full-time mother and wife. However, as soon as she gets her three children off to school, she begins to create beautiful oil paintings. This is not a fanciful pastime for Jakobsen. She is recognized as one of America's leading contemporary folk artists. She is also one of the most popular, with paintings in the permanent collections of the Smithsonian Institution, the Henry Ford Museum, the Museum of American Folk Art, and the Gerald Ford Presidential Museum.

With direction from her artist mother, Jakobsen began painting at age four. As an artist of twenty-one years, she has created more than 500 paintings and four children's books.

Jakobsen's interest in illustrating children's books started as she began sharing picture books with her young children. Her first commission was to paint illustrations for Reeve Lindberg's book *Johnny Appleseed* (Little, Brown, 1990). She then produced her own text and art for *Meet Me in the Magic Kingdom* (Disney Press, 1995), the story of families visiting Walt Disney World in Florida, and *My New York* (Little, Brown, 1993), the story of two young friends seeing the sights of New York City.

Soon after the publication of *My New York*, Jakobsen received a call from Nora Guthrie, daughter of the legendary folk singer Woody Guthrie. Nora Guthrie's own children loved the New York book. This telephone conversation led to a joint project between the Guthrie family and Jakobsen to develop a picture book based on Woody Guthrie's song "This Land Is Your Land."

"I felt very honored that I was sought out to help make this book a testament to an American legend's life," says Jakobsen. "I read and learned so much about this interesting and talented man from Okemah, Oklahoma. I spent many months of research time with a great deal of assistance from the people at the Woody Guthrie Archives in New York City."

This Land Is Your Land is a detailed visual of Woody Guthrie's travels, his beliefs, his family and friends, and his legacy. "I spent over 2,000 hours of painting time to create the illustrations," says Jakobsen.

The illustrator has created a book with a tremendous amount of color, detail, and activity. Close inspection of the paintings reveals much more than what at first seem merely scenes of daily life and places of interest. Readers will enjoy searching for Woody Guthrie in his black-and-red checked shirt. He can also be spotted on a beach building a sandcastle and with a friend on the top of a train. Guthrie's quotations in the small corner boxes give insight into the man who wrote every day of his life no matter where he was. On page 24 of *This Land Is Your Land*, Jakobsen includes a few of the people Guthrie influenced.

"I hope young readers will take to heart the message of the last verse of *This Land Is Your Land*," stresses Jakobsen. "YOU alone can stop yourself, so don't give up. Always try!"

Jakobsen will continue her personal goal "to create beautiful art for the soul and spirit."

This Land Is Your Land has been recognized as a Publishers Weekly Best Book, a School Library Journal Best Book, a New York Times Notable Book of the Year, and a Parenting Book of the Year.

The Jakobsen family lives in Connecticut. The illustrator's artwork can be viewed at www.wildapplegraphics.com. Write to Kathy Jakobsen through Little, Brown and Company, Time Warner Inc., 1271 Avenue of the Americas, New York, NY 10020.

Discussion Questions

Make sixteen photocopies of the guitar (Figure 15.1) on bright paper. Reproduce the questions (page 214) on white copy paper. Cut and glue them to the back of the guitars. Laminate, if possible, and cut along the outlines of the guitars.

Pass the discussion questions around in a small suitcase or duffel bag. Have one child select a guitar from the suitcase, read the question aloud, and give his or her opinion or answer. If desired, the discussion can be opened to the group for others to give their viewpoints or thoughts. Then the child passes the suitcase to the next individual who repeats the process. Allow only one guitar to be drawn at

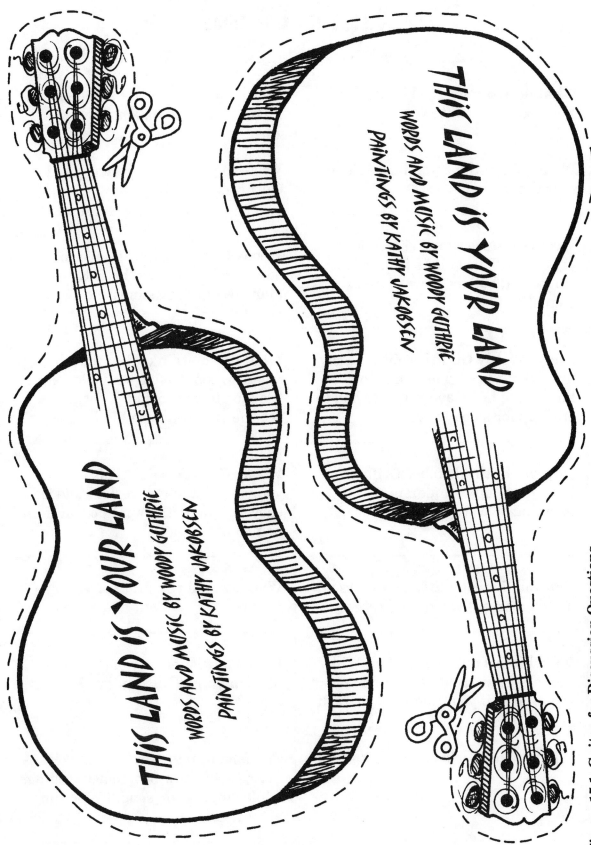

Figure 15.1. Guitar for Discussion Questions

Discussion Questions

What does the song "This Land Is Your Land" mean to you?	Do you have a favorite scene in *This Land Is Your Land*?
What is something you know about redwood trees?	What do you think of Woody Guthrie?
Woody Guthrie sang "This land is your land. This land is my land." How could both of those phrases be true?	Woody Guthrie said, "I have room for one more friend, and he is Everyman." What did he mean?
One of Woody Guthrie's favorite sayings was "Stick up for what you know is right." Have you ever had to stick up for something?	What do you think Woody Guthrie meant when he said, "I don't want the kids to be grown up. I want to see the grown-ups be kids"?
How did Kathy Jakobsen's illustrations help you to understand the meaning of Woody Guthrie's song?	Woody Guthrie said, "This world is your world and my world. Take it easy, but take it." What do you think he meant?
Can you find Gulf Stream waters on a land map of the United States?	Where would you find redwood forests?
Would it feel different to sing "This Land Is Your Land" with a large group than if you sang it by yourself?	Have you visited any of the places illustrated in *This Land Is Your Land*?
What makes a folk song a folk song?	The foldout pages in *This Land Is Your Land* show people doing things while singing the song. Name the activities.

a time. This prevents others from reading and concentrating on their questions and not listening to what is being discussed

Remember, some of the discussion questions have more than one answer, or there is no "right" answer. Children may voice a completely different response than expected.

Activities

The Places I've Been Activity Map

✓ **SUPPLIES**
8½-by-11-inch white photocopy paper
Crayons or colored pencils

Photocopy the activity sheet (Figure 15.2, page 216) for each child in the book club. Distribute crayons or colored pencils and direct the children to outline or color the states in which they have lived or that they have visited. For extended participation, the children can express which state they like the best and why.

This Land Is a Great Land Game

✓ **SUPPLIES**
Poster board (use a light color)
Markers or crayons

This is a fun, sharing activity for participants around a campfire (see "Introduction" for directions on making a fake campfire) or in a circle of chairs. If desired, write the introductory phrase (see below) onto a large piece of poster board and position it for all in the group to see.

The adult moderator will begin the game. Repeat the four lines of the introductory verse, name a place you have visited, and tell why you liked it. Each participant must first repeat the following verse before talking about a town or city, historical site, national park, or other place in the United States he or she has visited:

I've traveled America,
And what did I see?
Great people and places,
Just like Woody Guthrie.

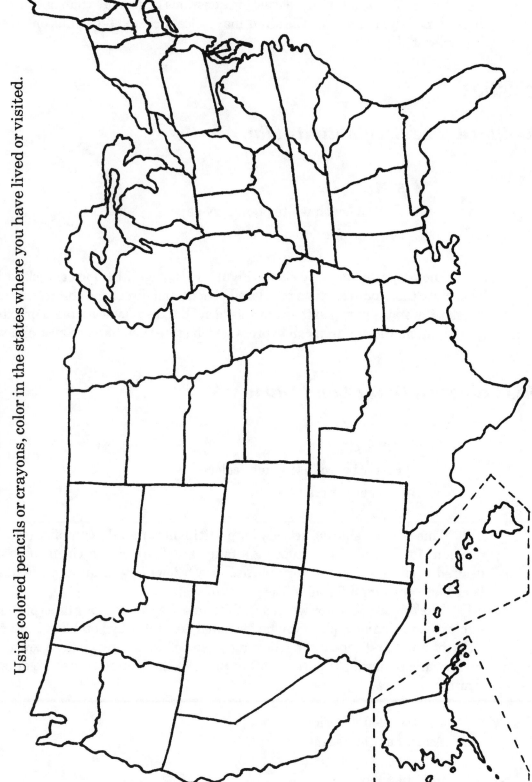

THE PLACES I'VE BEEN

Using colored pencils or crayons, color in the states where you have lived or visited.

Figure 15.2. The Places I've Been Activity Map

Craft

America Is Beautiful Travel Sticker Craft

✓ **SUPPLIES**

8½-by-11-inch white photocopy paper

Markers, crayons, or colored pencils

Yarn (a 6-inch length for each child)

Single-hole punch

Scissors

It was once a popular hobby for travelers to purchase stickers from places they visited and adhere them to their suitcases or car windows. Colorful labels from the Grand Canyon, New York City, Anchorage, or Paris brightened a traveler's carryall or advertised family auto trips.

Participants can create their own memories of places visited or locations they would like to someday see. Photocopy the travel sticker border (Figure 15.3, page 218) on white paper. Give the children markers, crayons, or colored pencils and instruct them to make a simple design or drawing within the border. Travel magazines, books on the United States and other countries, or a set of encyclopedias will help children with ideas on what to draw.

Today most travelers prefer to take suitcases constructed of cloth. To modernize the concept of travel stamps, laminate the finished products, punch a single hole at one corner, and tie them with colorful yarn to the children's backpacks or have the children take them home to tie to suitcases.

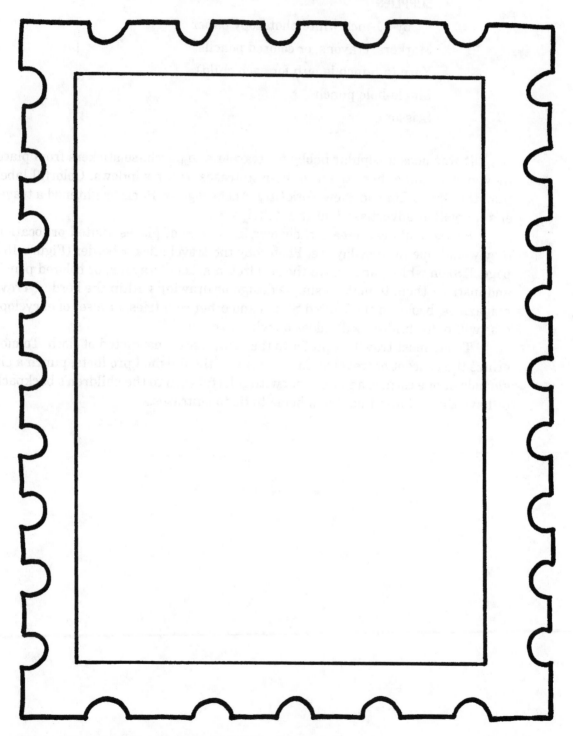

Figure 15.3. America Is Beautiful Travel Sticker

Snacks

Children can "eat" a part of Woody Guthrie's famous folk song—"From the redwood forests to the Gulf Stream waters . . ."

Redwood Tree Bark Brownies: Serve any kind of chocolate or fudge brownies. (Substitute with chocolate cookies or long rye crackers, if desired.)

Gulf Stream Water: Serve any blue-colored drink or purple grape juice. (Blue powdered drinks are available for purchase in grocery stores, or use blue food coloring in lemonade.)

Optional Supplies

— Small, brown paper bags
— Macramé cord
— Canteen or thermos
— Small paper cups
— Napkins

You may want to place "snacks for the road" into small, brown paper bags tied closed with macramé cord. These will portray travel knapsacks that Woody Guthrie might have used as he traveled the country. Consider pouring the refreshment drinks from a thermos or canteen.

Other Titles to Share

Ahlberg, Allan. *Mockingbird*. Illustrated by Paul Howard. Cambridge, MA: Candlewick Press, 1998. [23 pages]

Mockingbird is an endearing variation of the traditional lullaby "Hush Little Baby," one of several versions of this song in picture book format.

Bangs, Edward. *Steven Kellogg's Yankee Doodle*. Illustrated by Steven Kellogg. New York: Parents' Magazine Press, 1976. [34 pages]

Lyrics of the well-known song of the American Revolution are rearranged and decorated in Kellogg's style. Musical score included.

Bullock, Kathleen. *She'll Be Comin' Round the Mountain*. New York: Simon & Schuster, 1993. [31 pages]

The easy-to-sing American folk song is brought to life with lively illustrations. Musical score included.

Cooper, Floyd. *Cumbayah*. New York: Morrow Junior Books, 1998. [30 pages]

Cooper illustrates a well-known American folk song with artwork representing international ethnicities. Illustrator's note gives insight into the origins of the song. Musical score included.

Gershwin, George DuBose, Dorothy Heyward, and Ira Gershwin. *Summertime: From Porgy and Bess*. Illustrated by Mike Wimmer. New York: Simon & Schuster, 1999. [31 pages]

Text is based on the song "Summertime" from the folk opera *Porgy and Bess*. Wimmer's vivid oil paintings depict a family's summer activities. Musical score included.

Guthrie, Woody. *This Land Is Your Land*. Illustrated by Kathy Jakobsen. 12 min. Norwalk, CT: Weston Woods, 1999. Videocassette.

Weston Wood's visual treat brings the favorite folk song to life with the brilliant art of Jakobsen and the clear voice of Guthrie's son Arlo, as well as Woody himself. Includes a biographical segment about Woody Guthrie narrated by his daughter Nora.

Guthrie, Woody, and Marjorie Mazia Guthrie. *Arlo Guthrie and the Guthrie Family Sing: Woody's 20 Grow Big Songs*. Housatonic, MA: Rising Son Records, 1992. Audiocassette.

Digitally remastered to include the voice of Woody Guthrie along with his children and grandchildren. A collection of Guthrie's songs for children, including "Put Your Finger in the Air," "Jig Along Home," and "Howdy Doo."

————. *Woody's 20 Grow Big Songs: Songs and Pictures*. New York: HarperCollins, 1992. [48 pages]

This book can accompany the audiocassette tape by the same name. The songs were written by Guthrie and his wife Marjorie for their daughter and went unpublished for forty years.

Hammerstein, Oscar. *A Real Nice Clambake*. Lyrics by Oscar Hammerstein II. Music by Richard Rodgers. Illustrated by Nadine Bernard Westcott. Boston: Little, Brown, 1992. [27 pages]

An old-fashioned New England clambake is portrayed with lively illustrations. Lyrics taken from Rodgers and Hammerstein's musical *Carousel*. Musical score included.

————. *The Surrey with the Fringe on Top*. Lyrics by Oscar Hammerstein II. Music by Richard Rodgers. Illustrated by James Warhola. New York: Simon & Schuster, 1993. [26 pages]

Bright and animated pictures accompany the Rodgers and Hammerstein lyrics from the musical production *Oklahoma!* Musical score included.

I Know an Old Lady. Illustrated by G. Brian Karas. New York: Scholastic, 1994. [32 pages]

A cumulative English folk song tells a nonsense tale about a woman with odd eating habits. Musical score included.

Key, Francis Scott. *The Star-Spangled Banner*. Illustrated by Peter Spier. Garden City, NY: Doubleday, 1973. [52 pages]

Verses of the national anthem of the United States are illustrated in detail. Historical notes about the composer, how the song evolved, and the musical score are included.

Krull, Kathleen. *Gonna Sing My Head Off! American Folk Songs for Children*. Illustrated by Allen Garns. New York: Alfred A. Knopf, 1992. [147 pages]

A child-pleasing collection of songs that contains relevant and insightful notes of explanation about the music. Introductory note by Arlo Guthrie.

Medearis, Angela Shelf. *The Zebra-Riding Cowboy: A Folk Song from the Old West*. Illustrated by María Cristina Brusca. New York: Henry Holt, 1992. [32 pages]

A western folk song tells of a city fellow who proves he is not a greenhorn. Medearis provides information about African American and Hispanic cowboys. Musical score included.

Norworth, Jack. *Take Me out to the Ballgame*. Illustrated by Alec Gillman. New York: Four Winds Press, 1993. [32 pages]

These illustrations represent a World Series game from 1947. Music and original verses for America's favorite baseball song are included.

Seeger, Pete. *Abiyoyo*. Illustrated by Michael Hays. New York: Macmillan, 1986. [45 pages]

Singer/musician Seeger adapted this story from an old African folktale and has performed it on stage for years. Musical score included.

Time-Life's Treasury of Folk Music: An All-Star Hootenanny, Vol. 2. Hollywood, CA: Time-Life Music, 1996. Two compact discs.

Thirty folk songs on two compact discs include favorites such as "This Land Is Your Land," "On Top of Old Smokey," "Froggie Went a-Courtin'," and "John Henry."

Westcott, Nadine Bernard. *There's a Hole in the Bucket*. New York: HarperCollins, 1990. [23 pages]

Westcott creates humorous illustrations for this traditional folk song. Musical score included.

Younger, Barbara. *Purple Mountain Majesties: The Story of Katharine Lee Bates and "America the Beautiful."* Illustrated by Stacey Schuett. New York: Dutton Children's Books, 1998. [32 pages]

Katharine Lee Bates grew up to be a poet and a professor of English. During a trip from Boston, Massachusetts, to Colorado Springs, Colorado, she jotted down verses that would later become the song "America the Beautiful."

Contacting the Publisher

Contact the marketing department of Little, Brown and Company at Time Warner Inc., 1271 Avenue of the Americas, New York City, New York 10020, 212-522-8700, http://www.twbookmark.com. Ask what promotional items they have for *This Land Is Your Land* such as posters, bookmarks, and the illustrator's biography. Request enough supplies for each child in your book club and your files.

CHAPTER 16

The Tortoise and the Hare

By Janet Stevens

Stevens, Janet. *The Tortoise and the Hare*. New York: Holiday House, 1984. [32 pages]

In an endearing adaptation of the classic tale, a boastful rabbit challenges a turtle to a race, and with the aid of supportive friends, the results are anything but expected.

Introduction

Sharing Janet Steven's *The Tortoise and the Hare* will give children an opportunity to learn about the ancient history of the Olympic Games and a famous storyteller named Aesop. The first known Olympic contests took place in 776 B.C. in Greece. Held every four years, the games were meant to honor Zeus, king of the Greek gods. In the beginning, the Olympics were only for male contestants, and only male spectators were allowed to attend. The Roman Empire conquered Greece during the 100s B.C., and the quality and religious significance of the Olympics began to decline. Finally, the games were discontinued and not held again for 1,500 years.

The first modern-era games took place in 1896, with the hope that an international sports competition would promote world peace. Olympic competition is intended to test the skill and strength of individuals, not nations, and no scores are kept among competing countries. No nation "wins" the Olympics. Ancient Greeks honored victorious athletes with laurel-leaf crowns. Today, gold, silver, and bronze medals are awarded to champions.

Also long ago, in the country of Greece, a slave name Aesop was revered for his brilliant storytelling. His numerous stories contained lessons that were meant to teach fellow citizens better behavior. Two thousand years have passed and Aesop's fables are still relevant to modern society. Young readers enjoy these brief, simple, yet insightful, tales.

As with fables, rabbit and turtle stories have been a part of human culture for hundreds of years. In African and Native American folklore, the rabbit's cleverness constantly placed him in and out of trouble. In many parts of the world, the rabbit is the symbol of springtime, rebirth, and abundant life. In China and India, turtles are not only symbols of steadiness and patience, but also of health, wisdom, and long life. For this reason, they are often believed to bring good luck.

Note: A tortoise is a turtle that lives only on land. Tortoises have short hind legs that are different from the webbed feet of water turtles. Hares are often mistaken as rabbits, but they are larger and have longer legs and ears than rabbits. Hares do not dig burrows in the ground, as do rabbits.

Welcome the children to the session with taped music by John Williams, one of America's most famous composers. Williams has been creating bold and inspiring music for the Olympic Games since 1984. He composed and conducted "Summon the Heroes," a collection of music written for the Games that includes the official Centennial Olympic theme for the 1996 Atlanta venue (John Williams, *Greatest Hits 1969–1999*, Sony Classicals, 1999. Two compact discs).

For interactive musical fun, distribute kazoos and participate in a group rendition of the ABC Television's theme music for their coverage of the Winter and Summer Olympics. This tune is familiar to almost everyone. While the children are tooting their kazoos, ceremoniously place laurel leaf crowns upon their heads (see page 234).

Serve healthful snacks so that the young readers will be "in shape" for the upcoming activities and discussion. If there is contact with the children prior to this meeting, consider distributing the Olympic Medallions Activity Sheet (Figure 16.2) ahead of time. An entertaining show-and-tell could be part of the session as the children eat their snacks.

For an irresistible and laugh-filled program, have an area prepared for the Tortoise and Hare Races. See page 231. Emphasize that enthusiastic cheering and encouragement from spectators play a most important part of any competition.

The adult moderator should practice the technique of racing the poster board rabbit and tortoise, to better coach the children in their racing endeavors. The talent is in the simple wrist action of repetitive pulling and releasing of the string to make the figure move. All competitors, whether adults or children, are equally matched in this delightful event that demands no special strength or agility. As an extending activity for home, photocopy a set of tortoise and hare patterns (Figures 16.3 and 16.4) for the children so that they can have contests with their families.

An alternative to the Tortoise and Hare Races is the Olympic Rings Flag Craft (see page 236). This project can also be sent home as an extending activity.

Questions to aid in the discussion are included in this chapter. Consider reading aloud other adaptations or retellings, such as Jane Yolen's rhymed version found in *A Sip of Aesop*, Don Dailey's rendition in his *Classic Treasury of Aesop's Fables*, and Helen Ward's *Tortoise and the Hare* (see "Other Titles to

Share" in this chapter). It will be fun to ask the young readers which version they favor.

Give everyone a commemorative "On Your Mark! Get Set! Go!" bookmark (Figure 16.7) when the session ends. The pattern is included in this chapter.

Introducing the Author/Illustrator

Janet Stevens

Used by permission of Janet Stevens.

Janet Stevens, noted author and illustrator, would like for readers of *The Tortoise and the Hare* to come away with an important message: "Don't quit because something is hard; if you practice, you will get better at it."

"Look at the Tortoise," she expounds. "He was not a natural runner like [the] Hare. He had to train to get to the level of being able to even enter that race. Still, he took the challenge. He persevered, and he came out a winner."

As a young girl, Stevens had to work hard in her school studies. "My brother and sister were the shining students. I was just average, and not a great reader," she says.

"In my third-grade class there were reading groups named after birds. I was a Blue Jay, not a Cardinal, and the Cardinals were the fastest readers. I never really understood what reading was all about, that it could be fun and entertaining. Then it happened. I chose a book that turned me onto reading, a book that touched my heart. I checked *The Yearling* (by Marjorie Kinnan Rawlings) out of the library, and read it slowly, by myself, with no pressure. I laughed and cried, and felt like I was reading for the very first time. What was important was that I was reading—and liking it. From then on, reading became easier. The more I read the better a reader I became.

"I'm sure Tortoise didn't think of himself as a runner, but with lots of hard work and support from his friends he ran a race. Who would have believed that Tortoise ever would have even been in a race? Who would have thought that a Blue Jay could create books?"

Stevens's parents encouraged her artistic pursuits as she grew up. They bought art supplies and enrolled her in YMCA art classes, where she was the only child in a class of adults. Stevens said she did not stand out artistically in elementary school, but that she enjoyed art and practiced all the time.

"I believe art is a skill that can be learned. As I progressed in school my art definitely improved. In high school, my art teacher was especially supportive . . . his encouragement gave me the confidence to continue working on my drawing."

After earning her bachelor of fine art in 1975 at the University of Colorado, Stevens attended an inspiring workshop led by illustrator and author Tomie dePaola. He was so impressed by her work that he showed some of it to a publisher who signed her to an illustration contract. Her first book was a poetry anthology edited by Myra Cohen Livingston titled *Callooh! Callay! Holiday Poems for Young Readers* (Atheneum, 1980). Now, Stevens not only illustrates books for other authors but also writes and illustrates her own using a variety of media, such as pastel crayon, pencil, watercolor, and pen and ink. Her illustrations have also expanded into computer-generated art, with the help of Ted, her computer-wizard husband.

"I've realized that computer technology can be a real extension of one's artistic ability," says the artist. "My experimentation with technology began with *To Market, to Market* (Harcourt Brace, 1997) where I scanned photos to create the collage background. In *Cook-A-Doodle-Doo!* (Harcourt Brace, 1999) I scanned actual objects, such as a cheese grater, to create the textures on the characters.

"I've learned to realize the joy of writing, illustrating, and life in general. I'm passionate about my work. I wish that children today could be more involved in things that bring them joy versus just wanting to win the prize or get the 'A.' Don't give up on something if you want to achieve it. My career has come because of my desire to illustrate children's books. I've worked hard. I've persevered. Just like Tortoise."

Janet Stevens welcomes correspondence from young readers. Write to her home address in Colorado or send an e-mail message: Janet Stevens, 3835 Spring Valley Road, Boulder, CO 80304, RhinoInk@aol.com. She also invites readers to visit her Web site at http://www.janetstevens.com.

Discussion Questions

Make sixteen photocopies of the award ribbon (Figure 16.1) on blue paper. Reproduce the questions (page 228) on white copy paper. Cut and glue them to the back of the award ribbons. Laminate, if possible, and cut along the outlines of the award ribbons.

Pass the discussion questions around in a small basket. The award ribbons should be face up with the questions hidden from view. Have one child select an award ribbon from the basket, read the question aloud, and give his or her opinion or answer. If desired, the discussion can be opened to the group for others to give their viewpoints or thoughts. Then the child passes the basket to the next individual who repeats the process. Allow only one award ribbon to be drawn at a time. This prevents others from reading and concentrating on their questions and not listening to what is being discussed.

Remember, some of the discussion questions have more than one answer, or there is no "right" answer. Children may voice a completely different response than expected.

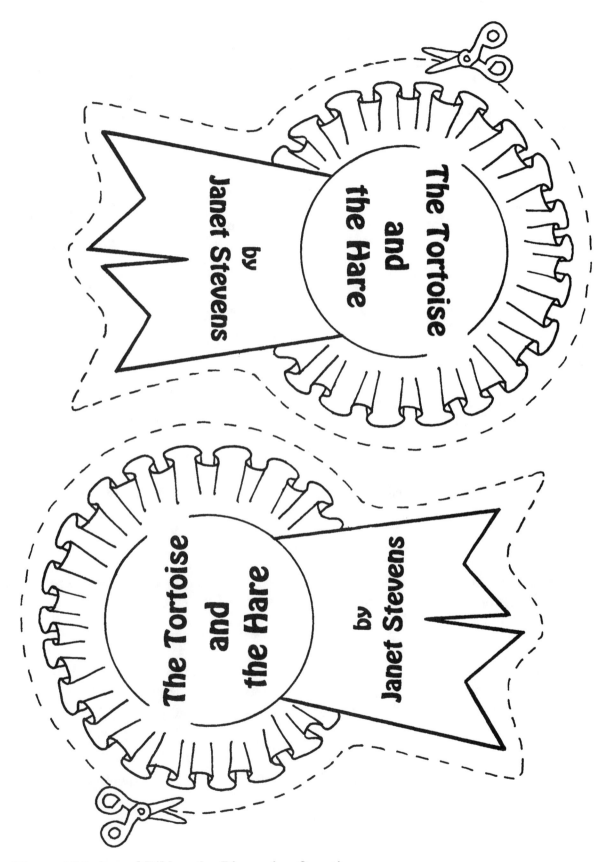

Figure 16.1. Award Ribbon for Discussion Questions

Discussion Questions

Have you ever given up on something? What happened?	Are you more like Tortoise or like Hare?
Is the turtle or tortoise really the slowest animal? Name some other slow creatures.	Have you ever been challenged by someone? What happened?
How did the running styles of Tortoise and Hare differ?	Would you rather be a scholar or an athlete? Why?
Did the tortoise win because he was lucky? Explain your answer.	What are some differences between a rabbit and a hare?
What are some differences between a turtle and a tortoise?	The hare was naturally a good runner. What is your natural talent?
Name your favorite sport in either the Summer or Winter Olympics.	Which sport do you think takes the most athletic ability?
What does the following mean: "It is better to have raced and lost, than never to have raced at all."	What are some animals that are faster than the rabbit or hare?
When you prepare for a test, do you have something for good luck? Do you have a lucky charm? What is it?	What does it take to get good at something?

Note: The slowest creature is the red slug, which moves only six feet per hour. The second slowest creature is the three-toed sloth, which moves a maximum of 518 feet per hour. The fastest land animal is the cheetah, which can run up to sixty miles per hour; the pronghorn antelope can reach speeds over fifty miles per hour. The fastest land birds are the ostrich and emu. They can race along at forty-five miles per hour.

Activities

Design Olympic Medallions Activity Sheet

✓ **SUPPLIES**

Options #1 and #3

— Pencils, colored pencils, and markers
— Yellow-gold photocopy or construction paper

Option #2

— Pencils, colored pencils, and markers
— Lightweight poster board (any color)
— Scissors
— Glue
— Single-hole punch
— Tricolored ribbon or yarn cut in 36-inch lengths
(one for each child)

Photocopy the activity sheet (Figure 16.2, page 230) on bright, yellow-gold paper. Ask the young readers to choose one of the options (see activity sheet).

For option #1 or #3, the children will use colored pencils or markers to create a medallion on the activity sheet. For option #1, the children will draw an Olympic event for an animal they like inside the lines of the medal. For option #3, the children will make an illustration for a sport that they would like to see become an Olympic game.

For the children who chose Option #2, provide lightweight poster board, scissors, pencils, and glue to create a stiff backing for the medal. In addition, provide either a 36-inch length of tricolored ribbon of red, white, and blue or a length of yarn so that the completed medal may be hung around the neck.

Children will first design a personalized medal with colored pencils or markers on the yellow-gold photocopy. Have the children cut out the medallion. Using a pencil, trace around the medal on the lightweight poster board. Cut out the medallion shape from the poster board. Adult assistance may be needed with younger children. Glue the yellow-gold photocopy medallion to the poster board and punch a hole at the top using a single-hole punch. Thread the ribbon or yarn through the hole and tie a secure knot.

Option 1: Design an Olympic event for an animal that you like.
Option 2: Design your own, personalized Olympic medal.
Option 3: Design a new sport you would like to see as part of the
Olympic Games.

Figure 16.2. Design Olympic Medallions Activity Sheet

Tortoise and Hare Races

✓ **SUPPLIES**

Scissors

Ice pick or sharpened pencil (adult use only)

White twine or box string cut in 10-feet lengths
(one length per child)

Masking tape

Crayons or nonpermanent markers

8-by-10-inch green poster board (one per child)

8-by-10-inch brown or tan poster board (one per child)

William Tell Overture recording (optional)

Using the patterns (Figures 16.3 and 16.4, pages 232 and 233), create several copies of the tortoise and hare templates for the children to trace.

Ask the students to trace and cut their tortoises from green poster board and their hares from brown or tan. Decorate both sides with crayons or nonpermanent markers.

When cutting out the tortoise and the hare, be especially attentive to the back feet—they provide good traction during the races. The adult moderator may want to cut the back feet for younger children.

The adult moderator will carefully punch holes where indicated by the patterns using a sharp pencil or ice pick. *Note: A hole puncher will make the opening for the string too large.* Cut a piece of heavy string ten feet in length for each participant. (Experiment with longer or shorter pieces of string depending on the space available.) Tie one end of the string onto a chair leg at twelve inches above the floor. If the knot on the chair leg slips, use a piece of tape to secure it. Thread the other end of the string through the hole of either the tortoise or hare.

Use masking tape to make one racing lane for each child. Have the children select either a hare or tortoise to race, and then trade animals for the next race.

Line up the chair legs so that they are even. Stretch the strings taut, then mark a starting line with masking tape. Begin with the poster board animals positioned upright with their back feet on the floor. A rough or carpeted surface makes for a faster track.

Using a repetitive motion of *gently* pulling the string back and then releasing it, the tortoise and hare will move along the string. It is necessary to keep the back feet on the floor. When the racers get to end of the string, a gentle jerk will flip them over for a return run.

Gioacchino Rossini's *William Tell Overture* makes great accompanying race music. (Gioacchino Rossini, *Favorite Overtures*, Stuttgart Radio Symphony Orchestra: Gianluigi Gelmetti. EMI Electrola GmbH, 1992. Compact disc.) The appropriate section of the overture, to play during the race, occurs during the last three minutes. Record this section twice on a cassette tape. Play the cassette tape recording when the race begins.

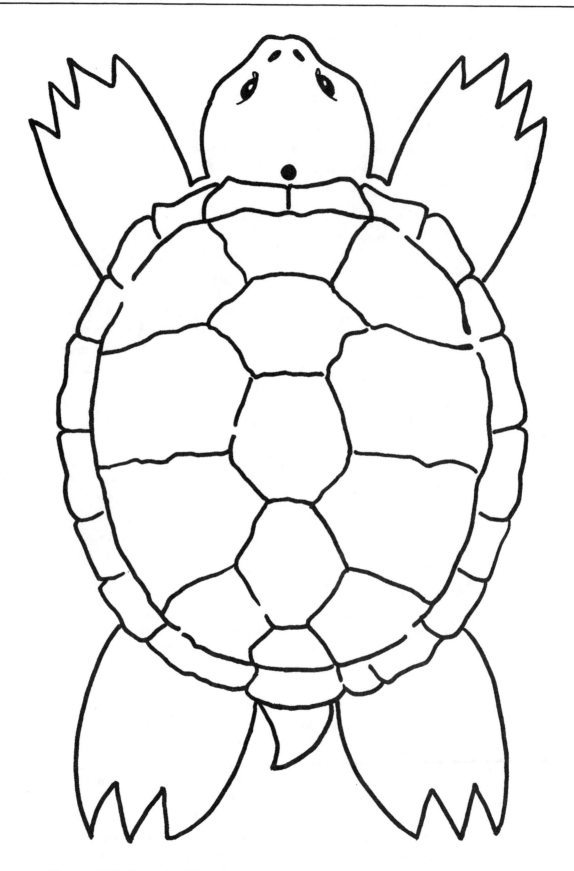

Figure 16.3. Tortoise Pattern

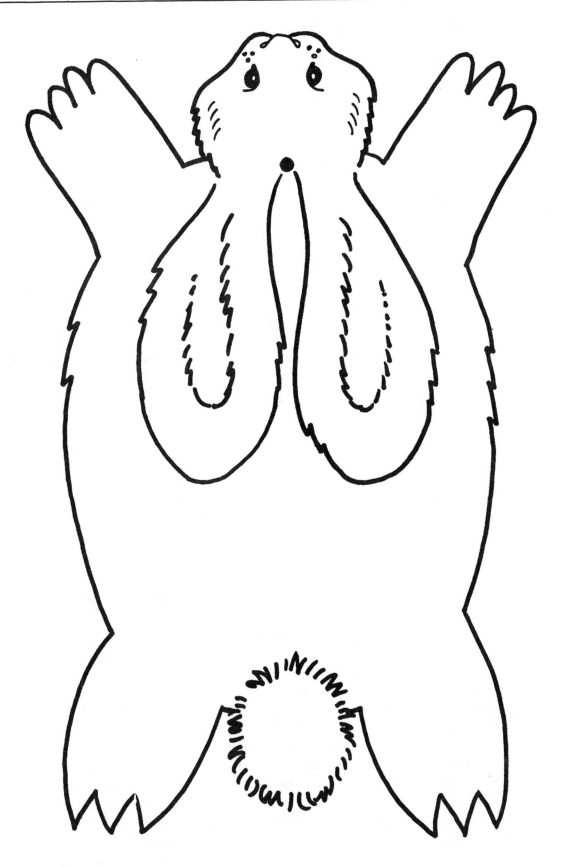

Figure 16.4. Hare Pattern

"On Your Mark! Get Set! Go!" Bookmarks

Photocopy the bookmark pattern (Figure 16.7, page 235) on colored tagboard, construction paper, or heavy art paper. Laminate, if possible, and cut along the dotted lines before distributing to the children.

Crafts

Laurel Leaf Crown

Figure 16.5. Laurel Leaf Pattern

Figure 16.6. Laurel Leaf Crown Sketch

✓ **SUPPLIES**

Green pipe cleaners (two per child)

Green 9-by-12-inch construction paper (one piece per child)

Poster board or cardboard scraps

The adult moderator will create a laurel leaf crown for each child to wear. Crowns are bestowed with pomp and circumstance at the beginning of the program (refer to the "Introduction" of this chapter).

Requirements for this craft are simple: two pipe cleaners and one piece of 9-by-12-inch green construction paper per crown. Using the laurel leaf (Figure 16.5), make a pattern using scraps of poster board from which to trace and cut. For each crown, cut twenty-four leaves from the green construction paper. Fold the paper in half, lengthwise, then in half again, and again. Trace three leaf outlines on the final 1½-by- 9-inch strip. Cut out the leaves.

Twist two pipe cleaners together securely. Carefully poke one end through the first leaf in the spot marked on the leaf pattern. Push leaf gently to the center, close to the twisted knot. Proceed with the other eleven leaves. Repeat the process from the other end. When finished, twist the two ends together, then space the leaves evenly around the circle. Now the children can wear their garlands, as did the victorious Olympians of Ancient Greece (see Figure 16.6 for an example).

Figure 16.7. "On Your Mark! Get Set! Go!" Bookmark

Olympic Rings Flag Craft

✓ **SUPPLIES**

White construction paper

Red, yellow, blue, green, and black construction paper

10-inch straws or dowel rods

Pencils

Glue sticks

Scissors

Cool glue gun (adult use only) or adhesive tape

The five interlocking rings of the International Olympic Committee's Olympic flag represent the continents of Africa, Asia, Australia, Europe, and the Americas and the meeting of athletes from throughout the world at the Olympic Games. Baron Pierre de Coubertin, founder of the modern Olympic Games, designed the flag in 1913. The flag of every competing nation has at least one of these colors.

Photocopy and cut one flag pattern (Figure 16.8) for each child using the white construction paper. Make several poster board templates of Figure 16.9, from which each child will trace and cut the five rings. Give each participant a sheet of red, yellow, blue, green, and black construction paper cut into three-inch squares. Demonstrate for the children how they will trace around the outside and inside of the ring. Then show them how to cut through the ring to cut along the inside line. See the ring pattern as an example of where the cut should be made.

Lay the rings on the white paper in the following order from left to right: blue, yellow, black, green, and red. The blue ring is the closest one to the flagpole. (Refer to a photograph of the Olympic flag in an encyclopedia for more information regarding specific placement.) Place the five rings along the middle in the center of the flag and open up the slits to interlock the rings together. Glue the rings into place on the flag. Using the cool glue gun or adhesive tape, attach the flag to a straw or dowel rod.

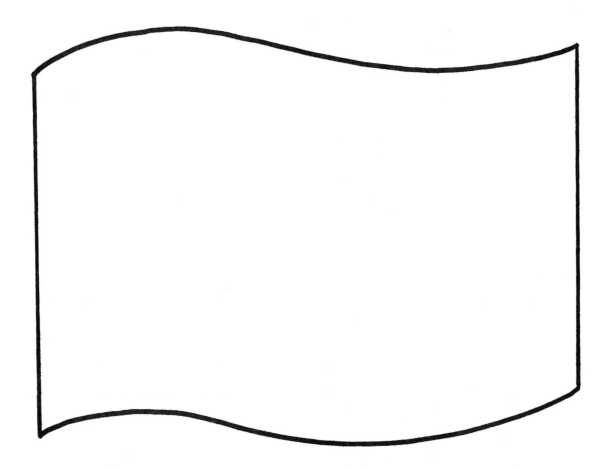

Figure 16.8. Flag Pattern

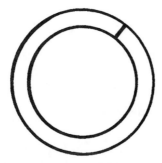

**Figure 16.9. Olympic
Ring Pattern**

Snacks

Sports drinks

Trail mix (recipe follows) or granola bars

Jelly bean "vitamins"

Orange, banana, and apple slices (chocolate or yogurt for
dipping are options)

Snacks are easy for this session. Serve a variety of healthful choices such a trail mix and fresh fruits plus something for the sweet tooth—jelly beans. Lemonade or fruit juice can substitute for the more expensive sports drinks.

Trail Mix

Note: Before serving, make sure none of your book club members have an allergy to peanuts or peanut dust.

Mix together the following ingredients (Makes twelve half-cup servings)

2 cups peanuts
2 cups raisins
2 cups sunflower seeds
2 cups of small chocolate candies (optional; increases servings to sixteen half-cups)

Other Titles to Share

Aesop's Fables. Illustrated by Michael Hague. New York: Holt, Rinehart and Winston, 1985. [28 pages]

Thirteen of Aesop's most well-known tales are retold and illustrated by this renowned artist.

The Classic Treasury of Aesop's Fables. Illustrated by Don Daily. Philadelphia: Courage Books, 1999. [55 pages]

A delightful, longer version of the tortoise and hare story is included along with nineteen other tales. Dazzling illustrations in an oversized format.

Coburn, John. *Turtles Today: A Complete and Up-to-Date Guide.* Philadelphia: Chelsea House, 1997. [65 pages]

With colorful, glossy photographs, all aspects of the turtle as a pet are covered.

Hinds, Kathryn. *Rabbits*. Tarrytown, NY: Marshall Cavendish, 1999. [32 pages]

> Abundant, distinctive photographs of hares and rabbits enhance the text, which describes habits, characteristics, and other interesting facts.

Hirschi, Ron. *Turtle's Day*. Photographs by Dwight Kuhn. New York: Cobblehill Books, 1994. [33 pages]

> Stunning, close-up photographs with simple text give a delightful insight into the existence of an eastern box turtle. The afterword touches on ancient beliefs about turtles and the importance of environmental awareness regarding them.

Mayo, Gretchen Will. *Here Comes Tricky Rabbit!* New York: Walker, 1994. [38 pages]

> Five stories from various Native American tribes are retold and illustrated by the author.

Middleton, Haydn. *Modern Olympic Games*. Des Plaines, IL: Heinemann Library, 2000. [32 pages]

> Gives an introduction to the history, athletes, rituals, events, and excitement of the Olympic Games.

Miller, Michaela. *Rabbits*. Des Plaines, IL: Heinemann Interactive Library, 1998. [24 pages]

> Rabbit facts combined with helpful pet information are presented for the younger reader.

Morley, Christine, and Carole Orbell. *Me and My Pet Rabbit*. Illustrations by Brita Granström. Chicago: World Book, 1997. [32 pages]

> All aspects of rabbits as pets are presented.

Parker, Steve. *Running a Race*. Photographs by Chris Fairclough. Illustrated by Hayward Art. New York: Franklin Watts, 1991. [32 pages]

> Visuals and text describe what it takes for the human body to walk, run, and jump. Activities, a glossary, and an index are included.

Pirotta, Saviour. *Turtle Bay*. Illustrated by Nilesh Mistry. New York: Farrar, Straus & Giroux, 1997. [26 pages]

> Two young Japanese children learn about sea turtles from an environmentally aware, elder man who is wise and full of wonderful secrets about nature. Includes beautiful pastel illustrations.

Ross, Gayle. *How Turtle's Back Was Cracked: A Traditional Cherokee Tale*. Illustrated by Murv Jacob. New York: Dial Books for Young Readers, 1995. [32 pages]

> Turtle's bragging gets him in trouble with a pack of wolves.

Seibert, Patricia. *Mush! Across Alaska in the World's Longest Sled-Dog Race*. Illustrated by Jan Davey Ellis. Brookfield, CT: Millbrook Press, 1992. [32 pages]

> The annual Iditarod Trail Sled Dog Race of Alaska is described in a storybook style filled with engaging facts.

Ward, Helen. *The Hare and the Tortoise: A Fable from Aesop*. Brookfield, CT: Millbrook Press, 1999. [39 pages]

Ward presents an entertaining new slant to the well-known fable. Illuminating illustrations show numerous animals that are integral parts of the story. A detailed, three-page key to the animals is included.

Yolen, Jane. *A Sip of Aesop*. Illustrated by Karen Barbour. New York: Scholastic, 1995. [32 pages]

Aesop's fables retold in rhyming verse. Illustrated with bright, bold paintings.

Contacting the Publisher

Contact the marketing department at Holiday House, 425 Madison Avenue, New York, NY 10017, 212-688-0085, http://www.holidayhouse.com. Ask what promotional items they have for Janet Stevens's *The Tortoise and the Hare*, such as posters, bookmarks, and the author/illustrator's biography. Request enough supplies for each child in your book club and your files.

Author/Title Index

Subject Index

from *Libraries Unlimited*

100 MOST POPULAR SCIENTISTS FOR YOUNG ADULTS
Biographical Sketches and Professional Paths
Kendall Haven and Donna Clark

Revealing the career histories of successful 20th Century scientists, this exciting resource offers students a wonderful research tool and words of advice from great scientists on launching a science career. Much more than a collection of biographies, this is an inspiring and practical tool for students interested in science careers. **Grades 7–12.**
Profiles and Pathways Series
xv, 525p. 7x10 cloth ISBN 1-56308-674-3

BULLETIN BOARDS AND 3-D SHOWCASES THAT CAPTURE THEM WITH PIZZAZZ
Karen Hawthorne and Jane E. Gibson

This illustrated how-to guide provides detailed instructions, supply lists, and variations for an entire year (including summers and holidays) of exciting displays. Easily adapted to any subject or budget, these bulletin boards and showcases—proven favorites for students in middle and high school—will also excite the imaginations of younger students. **Grades 5–12.**
ix, 147p. 8½x11 paper ISBN 1-56308-695-6

GOTCHA!
Nonfiction Booktalks to Get Kids Excited About Reading
Kathleen A. Baxter and Marcia Agness Kochel

Booktalks and support materials for more than 350 nonfiction titles are organized according to topics popular with young readers: "Great Disasters," "Unsolved Mysteries," "Fascinating People," "Science," and "Fun Experiments To Do." These concrete, classroom-tested ideas help you effortlessly present the best of children's literature in irresistible ways. **Grades 1–8.**
xviii, 183p. 8½x11 paper ISBN 1-56308-683-2

THE INTERNET RESOURCE DIRECTORY FOR K–12 TEACHERS AND LIBRARIANS
Elizabeth B. Miller

With its curriculum-driven organization, simple instructions, and a wealth of information, this guide is simply the best Internet directory available for educators. All previous site annotations are updated as needed, and double-checked for accuracy. **All Levels.**
*Call for information on most recent edition.

STUDENT CHEATING AND PLAGIARISM IN THE INTERNET ERA
A Wake-Up Call
Ann Lathrop and Kathleen Foss

Put a stop to high-tech and more traditional low-tech forms of cheating and plagiarism. Also, learn to recognize the danger signs for cheating and how to identify material that has been copied. Sample policies for developing academic integrity, reproducible lessons for students and faculty, and lists of helpful online and print resources are included. A must-read for concerned educators, administrators, and parents. **Grades 4–12.**
xiv, 255p. 6x9 paper ISBN 1-56308-841-X